Foul Deeds & Suspicious Deaths
In Jersey

An unknown convict 'clapped in irons'. Jersey, c.1909. Author's collection

Foul Deeds & Suspicious Deaths In
JERSEY

GLYNIS COOPER

Wharncliffe Books

Dedicated to the memory of all those
who have suffered on Jersey
through the centuries.

First Published in Great Britain in 2008 by
Wharncliffe Books
an imprint of
Pen and Sword Books Ltd
47 Church Street
Barnsley
South Yorkshire
S70 2AS

Copyright © Glynis Cooper 2008

ISBN: 978-184563-068-3

Typeset in Plantin by Concept, Huddersfield.

Printed and bound in England by CPI UK.

Pen and Sword Books Ltd incorporates the Imprints of
Pen & Sword Aviation, Pen & Sword Maritime,
Pen & Sword Military, Wharncliffe Books,
Pen & Sword Select, Pen and Sword Military Classics
and Leo Cooper.

For a complete list of Pen & Sword titles please contact
PEN & SWORD BOOKS LIMITED
47 Church Street
Barnsley
South Yorkshire
S70 2BR
England
E-mail: enquiries@pen-and-sword.co.uk
Website: www.pen-and-sword.co.uk

Contents

Acknowledgements

Grateful acknowledgements are due to the Société Jersiaise, Jersey Libraries, the Channel Islands Occupation Society, the staff of the museum at La Hougue Bie, and all the islanders who were so friendly and helpful; and gave up their time to talk about Jersey.

Thanks also to Rupert Harding at Pen & Sword Books and the editor of the series, Brian Elliott.

Introduction

The Channel Islands lie in the Bay of St Michel off the northern coast of France. There are two Bailiwicks (taking their name from the Bailiff in charge of each Bailiwick): Guernsey (which comprises Guernsey, Alderney, Sark, and Herm) and Jersey. The Bailiwick of Jersey is different to that of Guernsey because, principally, it consists of just Jersey, the largest Channel Island, plus a few reefs and islets of which Les Ecréhous and the Minquiers are the most notable.

Jersey has twelve parishes: St Ouen (pronounced St Wan); St Mary; St John; Trinity; St Martin; Grouville; St Clement; St Saviour; St Helier; St Lawrence; St Peter; St Brelade. The largest parishes are St Ouen and St Brelade in the west of the island; while the smallest ones of St Mary and St John border the northern coast and St Clement the south coast. All the parishes have a coastline, although that of St Saviour is an extremely narrow strip. St Helier is the 'capital' of the island and lies on the eastern side of St Aubin's Bay on the southern coast.

The island was a farming and fishing community for centuries whose inhabitants augmented their incomes with knitting woollen stockings and smuggling. Outside of the coastal area of St Helier much of Jersey is still a rural community. Farms, hidden valleys, lavender fields, quiet streams, old Norman churches, village inns, apple orchards, and flowers everywhere. There are however also the marks of modern change, some unwelcome, which the islanders have had to learn to accept. In the sleepy village of St Peter, by the old crossroads, a concrete hatch at pavement level proclaims itself St Peter's Bunker, an unwelcome reminder of the five years of the German Occupation.

For most people the name of Jersey is synonymous with thick rich cream, real yellow butter, delicious new potatoes, and the warm woollen garment of that name so indispensable in English winters. The island is also renowned for its 10 ft (3 m) high cabbages, the stalks of which are used to make walking sticks; 'black butter' made from apples and cider; and the Jersey Lily – both the flower and the actress Lily Langtry, a Jersey woman renowned for

Farmers' wives by a Jersey well in Trinity parish, c.1910. Author's collection

her beauty as much as her talent, who charmed King Edward VII and earned herself the nickname of the Jersey Lily.

In recent years Jersey has earned itself a reputation as a tax haven and the finance industry is big business. The tourist industry is also booming. The majority of visitors are English but there are also a surprising number of Germans, fascinated by the one tiny corner of the British Empire that the Führer managed to occupy for five years during the Second World War. The islanders have not forgotten the war, and they never will, for it is a part of their history etched firmly into their folk memory; but they recognise the need to move on and, believing that 'the sins of the fathers' should not be visited upon their children, put a smile on their faces and welcome their German visitors cordially enough.

Behind the façades, however, lies another Jersey. Until the tenth century Jersey belonged to France. The sandy beaches of Normandy can often be seen from Jersey shores and much of the

Cabbages 3 m high, grown on the Island. Jersey, c.1910. Author's collection

island's heritage, culture, folklore, customs and superstitious beliefs, has Norman French roots. The adjacent Celtic kingdom of Brittany also had an impact on Jersey's early history and the geographical location of the island, much nearer to France than to England, meant that often its history owed as much to French influences as to English influences.

Like Guernsey, the island is a 'Crown Dependency'. Gibraltar shares the same status. Crown Dependencies owe allegiance to the Crown, not to Parliament. They are dependent upon the protection of the Crown against foreign aggressors and they may not declare war on another country without the consent of the Crown. However, internally, Crown Dependencies are autonomous; and Jersey citizens have their own government; their own laws and legal system; their own health, education and social services; their own post office; their own coinage; and their own flag. Jersey, like its neighbour, Guernsey, also clings fiercely to its independence and

The grave of Lillie Langtry in St Saviour's churchyard. The actress and society beauty was known as 'The Jersey Lily'. The author

the special privileges granted to the island through an accident of history.

The currency on Jersey originated from the old Norman currency of 'livre tournois' that had units of livres, sols and deniers (LSD which were the monetary symbols used in the UK until decimalisation). In the 1830s this was replaced by pounds, shillings and pence but the old monetary symbols remained. An old measure of Jersey money was:

1 sou = ½ penny
520 sous = £1 sterling.

Consideration was first given to decimal currency in the island in the 1870s but it would be another century before it was adopted. Jersey mints its own money but this is not deemed legal tender outside the Channel Islands. The island has retained £1 notes and does not mint £1 or £2 pound coins.

English has only been the official language for about the last 100 years. Before this it was French. Historical and legal documents, books and newspapers written before 1900 are mostly in French. For centuries a 'patois', a language that is a curious mixture of French and English but neither one nor the other, was widely spoken on the island although this virtually died out during the latter half of the twentieth century.

The judicial and administrative systems are different to the UK. Deputies (MPs) are elected every five years. They are presided over by the Bailiff, an islander who is appointed, usually for life, by the Queen, and the Lieutenant Governor, who is the Queen's representative and who is chosen from the higher English military ranks to serve a five year term of office. Juries are not made up from members of the public but from Jurats who are elected for life. When the Court sits an 'Inferior Number' consists of the Bailiff and two Jurats while the 'Full Court' has seven to twelve Jurats and the Bailiff. The Royal Court on Jersey has an almost supreme authority. The main form of appeal against a sentence passed by the Court is to the Bailiff and he will usually support the Court.

Today it is difficult for English people to understand that, while Jersey might seem to be English, it is not English in the way that most UK citizens might believe it to be. English law is not valid on Jersey and ignorance of this fact is no excuse as several have found to their cost. English citizens have no rights to live or work on Jersey without being granted a license to do so; and the conditions of being granted such a license are strict. The Health Service is not free and there is no reciprocal health care scheme with either the UK or the EU. Consultations with a doctor, call out of an ambulance or hospital treatment must be paid for, no matter what the circumstances, although in recent years UK nationals have been granted free emergency medical care.

At the same time there is no British Consul on Jersey because the island is not 'foreign territory'. Like Guernsey, the situation is a bit 'Catch 22'; although the local Citizens Advice Bureau is willing to offer whatever help it can to English people who find themselves in trouble. When asked the question 'is Jersey English?' the answer is 'yes and no.'

It is, however, necessary to try and understand the complex nature of Jersey's situation and make-up in order to understand the background to the stories related in this book; the reasons for some of the crimes committed; and the nature of the foul deeds and suspicious deaths which happened there. There is a general cut-off date for crime stories of around 1910 so as not to offend 'living memory' or the sensibilities of those involved with the victims and perpetrators of more recent crimes. The sole exception to this rule is the Occupation (1940–1945) which is such an important and unusual part of Channel Island history that it cannot be ignored.

Jersey's foul deeds and suspicious deaths are different in several aspects from those committed on its sister island of Guernsey. There was a great belief in witchcraft on both islands but in Jersey there were far fewer witch trials and witches condemned to death were strangled before being burned at the stake. Guernsey preferred to roast them alive. There does not appear to be a tradition of werewolfery on Jersey although the island had plenty of '*troublesome yowthe*'. Faeries, their existence, powers, deeds, have a much lower profile on Jersey than on Guernsey. However, Jersey has its share of smuggling tales, privateers, tragic love stories and murders, though these appear to have much more of a continental nature about them. Jersey wasn't isolated to the same extent as Guernsey and this is reflected in their culture, their community and their crimes.

A Brief History of Jersey

St Ouen's Bay stretches along the whole of the west coast of Jersey while St Aubin's Bay takes up much of the south coast. To the north treacherous granite cliffs, with plenty of hidden caves and small coves, rise up to 460 ft (c.150 m) above sea level; while the east has a gentler coastline. The predominate granite of the island's composition, coupled with shale, sandstone and lava, indicate that there was a volcano somewhere fairly local in the far distant past. The hinterland of the island is rural and pretty, somewhat reminiscent of Cornwall.

Like Guernsey, Jersey is a slowly drowning land and something of the distant past of the island can be glimpsed among the inter-tidal rocky remains. Usually it is fairly easy to discern former coast-lines with the naked eye. It is said that a natural raised causeway, known as La Planche, led from the east of the island to mainland France, and that it was once possible to walk along it. At low tide the causeway can be seen as a darker line in the water. It would have been possible to walk to France from Jersey anyway during the last Ice Age which ended c.8000BC.

Something which lends credibility to the theory of walking this causeway is the evidence of very early inhabitation on La Cotte de St Brelade, a peninsular on the eastern side of St Brelades Bay. Worked flints and crude stone hammers together with remains of mammoth, woolly rhinoceros, deer and great elk have been dis-covered there on a site said to have been inhabited by Neanderthal man over 100,000 years ago. A site of similar antiquity lies at Cotte a la Chèvre in St Ouen. To date there are no other such early sites on the island, but there may once have been; now probably covered by either blown sand or the sea. The waters covered land which is now the English Channel c.7000–6500BC. Later Stone Age habitation sites have been found on the sea bed further to the north and it is more than possible that similar sites exist in the seas around Jersey.

Around 2000BC immigrants from the Iberian Peninsula (espe-cially the area which is now Portugal) began to arrive in Jersey and these people were the dolmen builders. This period was part of the Bronze Age when Britain and the Atlantic seaboard (north-west) Europe were part of a huge ritual landscape characterised by the dolmens, menhirs (standing stones), stone circles, cairn building and cursii (earthen banks which ran in long parallel lines often linking features and monuments).

Seven menhirs and eight dolmens are said to still remain on Jersey but the most impressive and well known is the dolmen of La Hougue Bie. This barrow, 180 ft (c.55 m) high, covers a passage grave of cruciform shape which contained the remains of at least eight people of whom two were female. Grave goods included flint tools, bones from sheep, ox and pig, beads, pottery and limpet shells. These items would have been placed in the tomb with the dead person in the belief that they would need them in the afterlife. The site has been dated to around 3500BC, the time of Stonehenge, but the feature takes its name from the Norsemen who swept down into Jersey over 4,000 years later. Hougue is said to derive from 'haugre', the Norse word for a burial mound. In later centuries the Church built two chapels on the mound in an attempt to Christianise this pagan site. The first, the Chapel of Notre Dame de la Clarté was built in the twelfth century while the Jerusalem Chapel dates from 1520.

However, it was the Iron Age Celts who made the biggest impact on Jersey. Although their culture (two phases known as Halstadt and La Tené) is said to have originated in the Austrian salt mining villages during the seventh century BC, the people were the descendants of a migration which had begun around 1000BC in south west Anatolia (modern Turkey) and swept northwards and westwards across Europe. Today there are said to be five remaining Celtic kingdoms: Wales, Scotland, Ireland, Cornwall and Brittany. Brittany lies adjacent to Normandy on the western coast of France. Islands held a fascination for the Celts, who revered water, and sometimes in Celtic mythology the Celtic 'otherworld' has been described as '... the islands far across and sometimes under the Western ocean ...' Drowning islands.

The Celts were a passionate, vibrant, artistic people who brought their iron working skills to Jersey with them. They worshipped a mother goddess, believing the mother to be the giver of life, and the 'trinity of fertility' (birth, death, re-birth) based on the agricultural calendar. Their major festivals were: Imbolc (Festival of the Lambs on 1 February); Beltain (May Day on 1 May); Lughnasadh (Harvest Thanksgiving on 1 August); and Samhain (Old Years Eve 31 October; their New Year's Day being

'Mother Goddess' standing stone near the statue of the Devil, close to Priory Inn.
The author

1 November). The Celtic Iron Age overlapped with the Roman period and the Romans gave Jersey its first known name: Caesarea. They also left behind them coin and bronze rings from the reign of Commodus (AD185) close to Pinnacle Rock in St Ouen's Bay.

In the wake of the departing Romans, Clovis, King of the Franks (AD481–511), conquered Northern Gaul in AD484 and Jersey was among the lands he added to his extensive dominions. Clovis was one of the most well known members of the Merovingian Dynasty of France which was said to be either closely linked with, or descended from, Mary Magdalene, after she fled from the Holy Land. He was baptised in AD496, having been converted to Roman Christianity by his queen, Clothilde, and it was under Clovis that the Franks converted to Roman Christianity.

Jersey however was converted to Celtic Christianity. Around AD525 some of St Samson's Christian followers had left the old Celtic kingdom of Cornwall to escape religious persecution and settled on Jersey, renaming it Angia/Agna. St Samson was the Bishop of Dol who brought Celtic Christianity to Cornwall, the Isles of Scilly and the Channel Islands. In the Scillies an island was named after him. On Guernsey a parish and an eleventh century church were dedicated to him. In Jersey a Celtic Church was established in his honour at St Helier. Somewhere between the Scillies and the Channel Islands St Samson became St Sampson as he is known on both Jersey and Guernsey.

It was in this same period, around AD540, that St Helier first came to Jersey. Helier was born, it is said, in Belgium, and there are various stories associated with his upbringing which show him to have been destined for the religious life even before his birth. When he reached manhood he was baptised by Marcouf at Nanteuil and came to Jersey with the older and more experienced Christian missionary, Romard. Helier chose a small island named Hermitage Rock on which to live that lay off the south coast and could be reached by a causeway at low tide. Here he built himself a small monastic cell known to this day as The Hermitage. From

The Hermitage built in memory of St Helier, close to Elizabeth Castle, c.1920.
Author's collection

there he could see the approach of the marauding bands of Norman pirates who frequently terrorised the island and he could warn the islanders in time for them to protect themselves. For fifteen years this worked well and the pirates were cheated of much booty. Finally, in AD555, they vowed to get their revenge. Being forewarned of this, Romard went to fetch help for Helier from Jersey. However, the pirates were too quick for him. They landed on Helier's small islet where they found him praying by the sea-shore. By the time Romard arrived with reinforcements he found that the pirates had beheaded Helier with their axes and had left his body lying where it had fallen on the sea shore with the waves washing over it. Marcouf subsequently founded a monastery in St Helier's memory on the island next to L'Islet where Elizabeth Castle would be built over 1,000 years later.

Bretons, Celts from Brittany, inhabited Jersey until the time of the Viking raids in the eighth to the tenth centuries. The Norsemen were wild and fierce and caused a good deal of grief to all the Channel Islands. In AD911 Charles the Simple of France, thoroughly fed up with the repeated attacks of one particular Viking chief named Rollo, drew up a treaty giving Rollo the province of Normandy and creating him Duke of Normandy in return for Rollo's promise to keep the peace. To strengthen his position and secure Rollo's loyalty Charles offered Rollo the hand of his daughter in marriage.

Possibly surprisingly for a bloodthirsty Viking adventurer, Rollo settled down and kept the promises he had made. He converted to Christianity and in AD912 was baptised Robert by the Archbishop of Rouen in the beautiful old cathedral of Evreux in Normandy. When Rollo died in 929, his son, William Longsword, became Duke of Normandy and he annexed the Channel Islands in 933. It was Rollo and his Viking descendants who laid down the basis of feudalism in the Islands and in the tenth century this worked well. Just over 100 years later, in 1066, William, Duke of Normandy, invaded England and conquered the country, earning himself the title of William the Conqueror for posterity. Through William the Channel Islands and England were then united under one monarch.

Jersey, like Guernsey, still clings to an ancient Norman custom that is regarded as nothing short of quaint and eccentric in the twenty-first century. If someone feels that his or her property or rights are being infringed by another person, he or she can invoke the *Clameur de Haro* (Haro being originally 'Aro' and a corruption of Rollo) and in '. . . the presence of two witnesses he or she must kneel and cry "*Haro! Haro! Haro! a l'aide mon prince! on me fair tort!*" and then he or she has to recite the Lord's Prayer in French . . .' The disputed property or right is then '. . . under the protection of the Queen [or King] and a court case must be brought within a year and a day . . .'

The king made grants of land in the Channel Islands called fiefs to his favourite nobility in return for military services. Each fief was held by a Seigneur whose home was the manor house. All the other inhabitants of a fief were the Seigneur's tenants even if they owned their own homes. Each tenant generally paid his rent or tithes in foodstuffs (grain, eggs, meat, etc.). The bigger fiefs had their own corn grinding mills which the tenants were obliged to use. Feudal courts were called Courts of Chief Pleas and were held on each fief. Stone seats used by these courts can still be seen on some of the fiefs. A custom which has survived down the centuries is the use of the Norman style brass milk churns made in jug shaped form with a handle and a lid. They come in all shapes and sizes, often marked with the old measures for liquids, and look more like a jug for sangria than a milk churn.

King John, or John Lackland as he was popularly known, per- haps for obvious reasons, was not the most able or popular of English kings. He was the bad King John of Robin Hood legend who ill-treated his subjects, lost the Crown Jewels in marshes off the Wash on the Norfolk coast, and had evil designs on Maid Marian. John, by rights, should not have been king, but his older and more able brother, Richard Coeur de Lion, was away for most of his time fighting in the Crusades, and John found himself as a sort of king-regent.

In 1204 he lost Normandy to the French which left the Channel Islands in the front line. John, anxious to retain the Islands as a base from which to attack France, offered the Islanders generous terms to remain loyal to the English Crown. After due consider- ation they agreed, and have remained so ever since. However, for almost 300 years afterwards Jersey (along with its sister Channel Islands) suffered badly, mostly from raids by the French, until in 1480 Pope Sixtus IV issued a Papal Bull granting all the Channel Islands the 'Privilege of Neutrality'.

Some 800 years later the Channel Islands still cling to their 'privileges'. These privileges were that the old Norman law was to remain unaltered and Jerseymen could not be tried by any court but the Royal Court on Jersey. However, many aspects of this ancient French domestic and legal system do not sit easily with the beliefs of the twenty-first century. Much of it is based on the idea of fiefs, which is that of a Seigneur with his group of underlings who are his serfs or servants to rule as he pleases, and has little to do with the democracy which most Western nations now take for granted. Citizens of countries within the European Economic Union are free to live, work and travel as they please within member states. The Channel Islands stand alone and proud outside this Union, their rules for those who wish to live and work in the Islands appear harsh and antiquated and often against basic human rights. Jersey at least has begun to realise that it is time for change, time to move on and embrace the modern world, and that there are distinct advantages to being a part of a Common Market with their European neighbours, rather than staying locked in a feudal timewarp.

Jerseymen were not required to undertake military service either but they would accompany their Duke to England or serve the King (or Queen) if called upon to do so. Today the English Sovereign and the Duke of Normandy are the same person; though Queen Elizabeth II is not called Duchess of Normandy, she is still the Duke. Jerseymen will swear allegiance to the English Crown but not to the English Parliament. This is an anomaly for since Cromwell's time power has been vested in Parliament and not the Sovereign and it is Parliament's decisions on foreign policy by which they must abide, not that of the Crown. Many have pointed out that the Queen is not just English; she is Queen of a United Kingdom. However, in 1204 there was no United Kingdom and King John was an English King and that is where Channel Island mentality remains.

French raids on Jersey continued throughout the thirteenth and fourteenth centuries but in 1337, following a takeover attempt from an unexpected quarter, that of David Bruce, the deposed Scottish king, Jersey decided that the time had come to construct proper defences for the island. To this end Grosnez was built in the north-west; Châtel Sedement in the north-east; and Castle of Gorey (then known as Mont Orgueil) was built on the eastern side of the island. By way of reassurance, in 1341 Edward III, who had fought the French himself, confirmed to all the islanders '... privileges, immunities and customs granted by our Forebears ...'

The ruins of Grosnez Castle in St Ouens Parish, Jersey, showing the perfect symmetry of its beautiful Norman arch gateway silhouetted against the sky, built c.1204. The author

It was not enough. The Castle of Gorey was taken in 1461 by French forces headed by Jean de Carbonnel and Jersey remained under French rule for seven years until 1468.

The French still considered Jersey as a part of the Îles de Normandie and they were not about to give up. Every time that the English and French were at war, which was then frequently, Jersey was caught in the crossfire. Only when Pope Sixtus IV issued his Papal Bull in 1480 granting 'Privilege of Neutrality' were the Channel Islands excluded from current and future hostilities between the French and the English. Jersey settled down to what the island hoped would be more peaceful times. The French however had other ideas. During the reign on Henry VII (1485–1508) Gorey Castle was threatened with betrayal to the French. Then in 1549 the twelve parish militia bands of Jersey defeated yet another French invasion and this led to the building of Elizabeth Castle on the St Helier foreshore during the reign of Elizabeth I (1558–1603). Sir Walter Raleigh, Governor of Jersey in 1600, gave the Castle its name.

Elizabeth Castle, c.1921. Author's collection

The unsettled period in English history during the later years of Henry VIII's reign, when he was busy changing wives almost more often than he changed his shirt and growing ever more bad tempered about it, followed by the pathetically short ineffectual reign of Edward VI (1547–1553) and the bloody burning years of Mary I (1553–1558), left Jersey pretty much to its own devices. Edward Seymour, brother of Jane Seymour, the only one of Henry VIII's queens to give him a son, was Governor of Jersey from 1537–1550.

Seymour was an ardent fan of the Reformation which wanted the elaborate rituals and beliefs of the Catholic Church replaced by simpler practices and a return to the original teachings of the Gospels. In 1548 he initiated the Chantries Act which closed all the medieval chantry chapels on the island, and confiscated payments for Mass said for the dead and candles lit in their memory. By 1562, shortly after the accession of Elizabeth I, Jersey was firmly Protestant, having become a refuge for the Huguenots fleeing religious persecution in France and having taken on board the teachings of John Calvin.

Jersey also found itself firmly caught up in what later historians would term 'the European witchcraze of the sixteenth and seventeenth centuries'. During the reign of Mary I one could be burned at the stake for heresy for just being a Protestant. In Elizabeth's reign the situation became reversed and the 'heresy' was a belief in the Catholic faith. In reality witchcraft was a charge levelled at people, mostly women, who either had healing skills and knowledge of herbal medicines or who had an unwise tongue and talked of things better left unsaid. Jersey was 'kinder' to its witches (if it could be called that) than its sister island of Guernsey in that the unfortunate victims were strangled before they were burned at the stake so that they did not suffer the agonies of being consumed alive by the flames. Although Jersey had just as strong a belief in witchcraft and its powers as Guernsey, there were far fewer witchcraft trials and executions in Jersey. No one has quantified the reason for this but being closer to the Continent made Jersey less isolated and perhaps more tolerant due to the numbers of refugees the island harboured.

Elizabeth I was possibly the greatest monarch England ever had and the kings who succeeded her had a hard act to follow. They assumed her powers and her glory without having her personality and her wisdom, becoming much resented in the process. Within two years of her death in 1603 the celebrated Guy Fawkes had tried to assassinate James I in the infamous Gunpowder Plot. He failed, a fact the English still celebrate every 5 November. Despite this, by 1640 England was embroiled in the Civil War. So close to Jersey across the water, the French watched in horrified and fascinated disbelief, wondering if the same thing could ever happen to them. It was little over 100 years since that splendid pair of kings, Henry VIII of England and Francis I of France, had met on the celebrated Field of the Cloth of Gold.

Remembering the promises that Jersey had made to King John four centuries before it might have been expected that the island would support the King without question. The Bailiff, Sir Philippe de Carteret, although loyal to the king, nevertheless wanted Jersey to remain neutral. His nephew, Sir George de Carteret, was arms running from France through Jersey to the West Country, a Royalist stronghold, in support of the king, Charles I. The de Carterets however were much resented in Jersey at the time because they regarded themselves as the hereditary rulers of the island. Islanders' resistance, based on local issues with Sir Philippe rather than disloyalty to the king, forced Sir Philippe to take refuge in Elizabeth Castle while his wife took up residence in Mont

Orgueil (Gorey Castle). From their respective castles, the pair fired on Parliamentarian ships and received supplies by sea. After this the islanders' resistance melted away and, finally remembering its promises made to the long dead King John, Jersey declared itself firmly Royalist.

To the island's amazement and astonishment, however, its sister island of Guernsey remained firmly on Oliver Cromwell's Parliamentarian side throughout the Civil War and acquiesced in the beheading of Charles I in 1649. Oliver Cromwell's 'reign' turned out to be brief. He died in 1657 and was succeeded by his son, Richard, following the same principles of the system Cromwell had fought so hard to overturn. Richard Cromwell was a much weaker character than his father with no taste for the role he was asked to take on and within three years Charles II was restored to his throne. Charles had stayed on Jersey and it was while he was at Elizabeth Castle that he gave Sir George de Carteret the lands on the coast of Virginia which Sir George named New Jersey. Guernsey apologised abjectly for its disloyalty and was forgiven by the newly restored king. However, Jersey, conveniently forgetting its initial resistance to the Royalist cause on the grounds that it was due to personal dislike of the de Carterets and not disloyalty to the king, did not forgive Guernsey its treachery so easily and it marked the beginning of a friction between the two islands which has lasted to the present day.

The 200 years following the Restoration were years of enormous prosperity for Jersey. In 1688 there was a brief glitch when an attempt was made to seize Jersey for the deposed James II but it failed dismally and the Catholic regiments within the island were disarmed. Jersey supplemented its traditional occupations of farming and fishing and the knitting of woollen stockings with smuggling, or 'free trade' as it was known. There were also several shipbuilding yards to cater for the demand for ships at the height of the privateering era. Privateer ships (that is ships privately built and owned by one family or a group of families) had royal letters of permission on royal headed notepaper (Letters of Marque) to attack any enemy shipping. Though the Hanoverian monarchs had specified France (still looking to attack the Channel Islands) and Spain and their allies as the specific enemies of the English Crown, many of the privateers took these letters as carte blanche to attack whomever they pleased. When George III protested and took them to task the privateers began to attack English shipping as well.

There was of course still an ever present threat from the French. In the second half of the eighteenth century a number of defensive watch towers were built around the coast of Jersey as part of a defensive plan worked out by the Jersey Lieutenant-Governor Conway. These distinctive circular towers had three levels. The ground floor was for storing arms, ammunition and provisions; the second storey served as accommodation for ten men and one officer; and on top of the tower was a gun platform. Of the thirty-one towers built, twenty-four survive.

Conway was proved to be right in his fears of French invasion. On 6 January 1781, Baron de Rullecourt attempted another French invasion of Jersey. Landing secretly at La Rocque in the south-east corner of Jersey, he led a small invasion force to St Helier. There he awoke the Lieutenant-Governor and conned him into believing that he had a much larger army than he really did and advised the Lieutenant-Governor that he should surrender immediately. He might have got away with it had it not been for one Major Francis Peirson who simply did not believe de Rullecourt's claims. Major Peirson rallied his troops and fought de Rullecourt

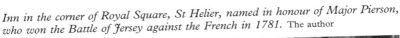

Inn in the corner of Royal Square, St Helier, named in honour of Major Pierson, who won the Battle of Jersey against the French in 1781. The author

The Battle of Jersey, fought in Royal Square, St Helier, in 1781. Author's collection

in the short but decisive Battle of Jersey which took place at Royal Square in St Helier. The French were defeated and slunk away with their tails between their legs. Many bodies are said to still lie buried beneath the Square. Both Baron de Rullecourt and Major Peirson were killed in the fighting and the Major's death was commemorated in a painting by John Copley which today hangs in London's Tate Gallery. In 1782 Seymour Tower, square, unlike the others, was built off La Rocque Point at the place where de Rullecourt had landed.

In 1789 it was England's turn to watch in horrified and fascinated disbelief as the French Revolution overthrew the old order and introduced the Reign of Terror. Those of the aristocracy who could, escaped. Those who couldn't faced the horrors of the guillotine or incarceration in the much feared Bastille prison. Napoleon glared at Jersey lying across the water and declared it to be 'a nest of brigands'. Plans were speedily drawn up for improving the island defences and Fort Regent was built in 1814 on the hillside above St Helier. In the event it was never needed.

'Le Don Hilton' was gifted to the National Trust in 1936 by Marie Hilton, built in 1756 as a guard house and powder storehouse. It was whitewashed in 1817 as a landmark for sailors and became a vraic gatherers cottage in the late nineteenth century; and a holiday home after the First World War. The author

Napoleon had greater issues to resolve and, fortunately for Jersey, never found the time or the opportunity to attack the island.

The Battle of Jersey turned out to be the last official French invasion of Jersey and the victory at Waterloo in 1815 marked the end of Jersey being a 'front-line outpost'. Today, however, over 200 years later, the French still look on the Îsles de Normandie, as they persist in calling them, as somehow remaining their own. Although Jersey owes allegiance to the English sovereign, has adopted English as its official language, and is now rather more English than French in outlook, the French never give up. Every few years French fishermen land on the Minquiers (known locally as the Minkies), a small group of virtually deserted rocky islets off the coast of Jersey which have good fishing grounds, and declare that they are re-taking the Bailiwick of Jersey for France. They are seen off good naturedly enough these days. Everyone just accepts that the French will not rest until the Îles de Normandie are once again their own; but it seems that they are going to have a long wait.

The one invasion which marked Jersey more than any other throughout its history was not French. It was the German Occupation of 1940–45. The Occupation was mostly not as physically brutal to the Islands as earlier invasions but it was a tremendous psychic shock to the islanders who were unable to defend themselves and simply had to endure whatever the Germans dished out. Hitler had declared that the Occupation should be 'a model Occupation' so that everyone could see that life under the German flag would be fine when Germany, as he misguidedly believed, ruled the world. Paranoid that the British would re-take the one corner of their empire which he had managed to conquer, Hitler ordered that Jersey, like the other Channel Islands, should be turned into an 'impregnable fortress'. Coastal bunkers, anti-tank walls, observation towers, artillery batteries, bomb proof barracks and a network of underground tunnels were to be constructed. Slave labour from Europe, mostly captured Russians, Spanish Republican freedom fighters exiled and stripped of their nationality by General Franco, Poles, Dutch and French prisoners from occupied European countries, were forced to build the ugly concrete structures. Most were left standing after the War, both as historical features and as a reminder of what must never be allowed to happen again.

The majority of Jersey folk stayed on their island for the duration of the Second World War. About 10,000 were evacuated to England just before the German invasion. These were mostly children, mothers of babies or toddlers, and young men of fighting age who could be recruited into the Forces. Several hundred Jersey men and women were imprisoned in camps on the Continent for misdemeanours or retaliations. Most survived; but some didn't. The Jersey Bailiff, Alexander Coutanche, intervened on behalf of those who fell foul of the Germans and pleaded their cases with an appreciable level of success.

Jersey may have acquitted itself better during the War than some of the other islands. All the wartime records for Jersey were released under the fifty year rule during the 1990s. Some of Guernsey's war records and all of those for Alderney are, unusually, embargoed for 100 years by Her Majesty's Government without explanation. Jersey has certainly begun to come to terms with the Occupation better than its fellow islands. The Liberation Sculpture on Liberation square commemorates the citizens of Jersey and their endurance of and liberation from the Occupation. There are also memorials to slave workers and other foreign nationals, notably the bunker memorial at La Hougue Bie, who suffered and died at the hands of the Germans on Jersey. There are no similar public memorials on the other Channel Islands who appear to be much more in denial than Jersey about what really happened.

In the years since the Second World War Jersey has become a haven for tax exiles. The finance industry is booming and some seriously rich people live on the island. Recently however the International Monetary Fund (IMF) put a spoke in the wheel when it announced that it was unfair practice not to tax businesses which only had their registered office on the island while businesses that actually operated on the island were fully taxed. Consequently, Corporation Tax was abolished for all businesses except those in the finance sector who must pay a uniform 10 per cent. In the shorthand language that has become so popular in the technical age, this policy has become known as 'zero-10'. This new policy takes effect in 2008 and it will leave a large hole in the States of Jersey finances. To combat this the island is set to introduce its first ever sales tax, more popularly known as VAT.

An ornamental clock in the centre of St Helier reflects the new industry of Jersey and the source of the Island's wealth. The author

The tourism industry however is also booming. Jersey is a pretty picturesque island which has echoes of Cornwall about it. The popular television detective series *Bergerac*, which was set in Jersey, did much for its public image, and visitors flock there every year. Each summer Jersey puts on its 'Battle of the Flowers' which is a stunning spectacular show of colour, design and imagination, not to mention hard work. Floats, tableaux, models, animals, are all made out of thousands of perfectly formed petals which must all be done within twenty-four hours of the flowers being picked. One of the highlights of the 2007 'Battle' was an authentic looking giraffe made entirely from flower petals.

Jersey has also been home to several writers and artists. These include the renowned Victorian painter Sir John Millais, the famous French writer, Victor Hugo (who lived in St Clement and saw visions of God there), and the twentieth-century writer and naturalist, Gerald Durrell, whose zoo is a popular feature of island life; but the island's most well known daughter was the renowned actress Lily Langtry, who was the daughter of a St Saviours rector and who married twice in St Saviours Church. Lily Langtry was the society beauty who captured the heart of King Edward VII. Although she spent her final years in Monaco she never forgot

The original model of the car used in the Bergerac *television series, Tiger Park, St Lawrence.* The author

The original model of the car used in the James Bond film Goldfinger, *Tiger Park, St Lawrence.* The author

her native island and her request to be buried in St Saviours churchyard was readily granted.

In 2004, to commemorate 800 years of Island loyalty to the English Crown, Gordon Young produced a sculpture in the form of a granite column inscribed with the 1698 Le Geyt Code of Law which lists crimes committed and punishments given. The column is topped by a stone toad (crapaud) which has been the symbol and nickname of Jersey folk for centuries. This derives from the small toads which used to inhabit the marshes and sand dunes of the area. The former habitat of these little creatures has now almost disappeared under modern development and their numbers have declined dramatically. The column is dramatic and stands at Charing Cross in St Helier.

St Helier today is a large bustling port and has changed almost beyond recognition from the small harbour town that Jersey's ancestors, and even nineteenth-century folk, would have known. A small train chugs along the vast expanse of beach that is St Aubin's

Le Geyt Law Column, built in 2004, topped by a Jersey toad (crapaud), Charing Cross, St Helier. The author

Bay up to the town of St Aubin. The Jersey Airshow is held here in the summer. Buses run from Liberation Square to all points of the Island. There is a big modern airport in St Peter's parish. Much of the rest of the Island however would be very recognisable to those who have gone before. The small northern parishes of St Mary,

St John and Trinity have changed little over the centuries. There are parts of St Mary where it is almost possible to imagine the couple riding on horseback down the green lanes to their clandestine marriage in the little chapel of St Mary de Lecq (Chapter 9). Jersey is a pretty island; the islanders are friendly and helpful; and there is a real sense of moving forward into a future that will be bright and prosperous for them.

CHAPTER 1

A Charge So Horrid
1299

*Renaud 'despoiled' her on a number
of occasions to 'teach her a lesson' ...
when she was finally released she was
bleeding and hysterical.*

I f there is such a thing as a 'designer' crime, then in the late thirteenth century it appeared to be the abduction and rape of Jersey women. The Jersey Assize Roll of 1299–1300 records an astonishing number. The perpetrators were rarely brought to justice because of a legal loophole and they became quite outrageous in their audacity. The rapes and abductions were not results of 'date rapes' or simply of having had too much to drink. They were planned and executed with the use of deliberate force and violence, with a complete and callous disregard for the female sex. The cases below represent only a fraction of those brought to the Court on 'a charge so horrid' that the details were not made public.

Peronelle de la Haye, the wife of Guillaume de la Haye, was at home preparing some supper for her husband who was due to return shortly from his toil in the fields. She was tired and she knew that her husband would be as well. After he had eaten they would go to bed. Hearing a noise, she looked up to see two men standing in the cottage. She knew them. It was a small enough community and everyone knew everyone else. Guillaume Baillehache and Jourdain Renaud stood there looking at her in a calculating and patronising fashion. Then Baillehache said that she was to come with them at once to answer charges of theft. Peronelle knew their reputation and she also knew that she was innocent. She refused to go until her husband returned, she said, and they had explained their accusations to him. The two men just laughed. Then they dragged her, terrified and screaming for help, to Baillehache's house where they accused her of having stolen a silver buckle from the house some days previously. She denied this vehemently but her abductors were not about to be deprived of their prey. Ignoring her screams of protest, Baillehache stripped Peronelle naked and announced his intention of 'despoiling' her as a punishment. She was then kept naked and imprisoned in his house for two nights and a day during which time both Baillehache and Renaud 'despoiled' her on a number of occasions to 'teach her a lesson'. When she was finally released she was bleeding and hysterical. Her outraged husband, Guillaume, at once invoked the Clameur de Haro (see A brief History of Jersey above) and, unusually, on this occasion Baillehache was actually arrested and fined ten shillings by the Royal Court.

Jeanne Corbel was not so lucky. She was at home with her mother, quietly sewing by the small turf fire, when Jean de Barentyn and Raoul Turgys broke into their house, smashing the door aside, and, without explanation, seized Jeanne. Jeanne screamed and struggled for she knew them and she had a good idea of what was about to happen to her. Her mother rose from the bench where she and Jeanne had been sitting and tried to protect her daughter but de Barentyn and Turgys were having none of that. Jeanne's mother was pushed aside roughly and one of them deliberately broke her arm to put her out of action. Jeanne managed to struggle free and crawled to her mother's side but again she was grabbed. Like Peronelle, the girl was stripped naked and, as her mother lay moaning and injured on the floor, Jeanne was 'carried off' to Longueville Manor. Here, both men 'committed other outrages against her' before she was discarded to make her way home as best she could. Jeanne was devastated and she also invoked the Clameur de Haro but with remarkable sangfroid de Barentyn and Turgys denied the whole thing and 'put themselves for life and death on the country'. This was an extremely serious oath to make, and the jurors, their palms well greased with suitable bribes, '... declared on their oath that they are not guilty and may therefore go quit thereof ...'

Free to look for fresh victims, de Barentyn's eye now fell upon another lady named Jeanne, the daughter of Pierre Renaud. Jeanne had married a man named Laurent Laysel, and it seems to have been a happy and contented marriage. The couple were at home together when a number of men burst into their house without warning. According to the charge, Jean de Barentyn and his friends, Guillaume de Tailleur, Guillaume le Warener, Geoffroi Langleis, and Henri le Palefraiur, then '. . . carried off Jeanne, wife of Laurent Laysel, against his wish and in his presence, and Jean worked his way with her . . .' After he had finished with her he turned over to his companions who also 'worked their way' in turn with her. When the distraught Jeanne was finally returned to her husband, he too invoked the Clameur de Haro. Once again de Barentyn and his friends denied everything, made their oath, bribed the jurors and were declared not guilty. A furious Laurent promptly sued them for rape. However, as the men had already been declared not guilty of these charges Laurent was sent to prison instead for defamation of character.

While Laurent was languishing in prison the five men were once more charged with rape, having 'carried off Colette, the mistress of Jourdain Brisbarre, Alice, wife of Viel Vasset . . .' and again the hapless Jeanne Laysel as revenge for her husband having dared to accuse them of rape. The men 'took them to the house of Drouet de Barentyn who worked his will upon them . . .' Once Drouet de Barentyn had sated his appetite the three women were then 'thrown to the wolves' and gang raped by the men who had seized them. Needless to say, Jean de Barentyn and his henchmen again 'put themselves for life and death on the country' and once more they were acquitted of any wrongdoing as the jurors again '. . . declared on their oath that they are not guilty and may therefore go quit thereof . . .'

It is impossible for those brought up in a world of equal rights for women to fathom the mindset of the thirteenth century, its 'legal eagles' and the Jurors of the Royal Court; but is probable that principles had nothing to do with it because for centuries money has talked louder than anything else. In addition, the accused were powerful men who could make life very miserable for those who crossed them. The women simply had to live with their shame and distress, and any resulting injuries or offspring, as best they could. In many ways it was a rather brutal time to be female and alive and living on Jersey.

Part of the problem was that Drouet, or Drogo, de Barentyn was the Seigneur of Rozel. It was his 'fief' and his 'fiefdom' and all the tenants were beholden to him. He also owned several other manors on the island and he was a powerful man. Together with his brother, Jean, their sons and their friends and employees, they roamed Jersey, fearing none and feeling free to do exactly what they liked. The islanders they injured were free to seek justice but they rarely got it (see also Chapter 2). Most court officials were either afraid of repercussions or susceptible to bribes and the de Barentyn family continued plundering the island and attacking its inhabitants with virtual immunity. The whole story simply confirms the saying that power corrupts.

Crime Does Pay
1299

Drogo's henchmen dragged them out and viciously assaulted them ... both of Thomas's arms were broken.

Drogo de Barentyn was the Seigneur of Rozel. Wealthy and powerful, he also had a number of other manors in his possession including Samerès and Longueville. His endless list of crimes in the records of the Assizes at the end of the 1200s would read comically if it wasn't for the tragic human side of the suffering he caused. The problem was that the system of justice on Jersey at that time was based on Norman law (as much of Jersey law still is) which required a jury of six men from each parish where cases were tried. Therefore neighbours sat in judgement upon neighbours. Each parish had its own Seigneur and no-one was going to give judgement against their own Seigneur if they knew what was good for them. Drogo de Barentyn and his brother, Jean, were therefore extremely powerful men and they used their power to help themselves and their friends to get away with abduction, gang rape (see Chapter 1), extortion, robbery and even murder.

There were plenty of civil cases where Drogo had helped himself to land that was not his by right and had retained wheat after the harvest which was not lawfully his to hold. He was even sued in France but when he was found guilty he just paid the fine and shrugged off the complaint. The warping of justice by Drogo de Barentyn in these civil cases is well illustrated by the case of Gaudin Karrere and Nicolas Warclipeys. They accused Drogo of seizing their lands in St Martin's Parish. He claimed that the lands were forfeited because of criminal acts committed by the complainants and requested a judgement. The two men claimed that they had received the King's pardon and produced the documentation. However, Drogo was acquitted, their lands were not restored and they were fined for making a false claim.

The criminal cases were even worse. Drogo and Jean de Barentyn had a number of friends, some of whom were employees, such as their warrener and their tailor. Guillaume de Tailleur, Guillaume le Warener, Geoffroi Langleis, Henri le Palefraiur, and Raoul Turgys joined the de Barentyn brothers in several escapades and also indulged in a few of their own. Guillaume le Warener attacked a couple '. . . on the King's highway at night . . .' He forced Richard Dovenand and his wife to take him to a tavern '. . . to their grave inconvenience . . .' and pay for his night out. As in the story *A Charge So Horrid* (Chapter 1) Guillaume simply denied the offence, requested judgement and was acquitted.

Le Warener also made a practice of taking and holding animals during the Banon (an annual period of free grazing rights) from common land or their owner's land and demanding payment for their release. He was tried and actually briefly imprisoned but on his release he started cattle rustling, fencing off common land and exacting tolls from people passing through, beating them up if they refused to pay. Eventually there were so many complaints that even Drogo got fed up and banned everyone from grazing their animals on his estates at Rozel, even during the Banon. Guillaume then turned his attention to impounding cartloads of vraic in Rozel harbour from a man named Jean Dalet who was told that it was illegal to land vraic at night. Dalet attempted to recover his vraic and was fined by the Seigneur, Drogo de Barentyn, for trespass and attempted robbery.

Jean de Barentyn's son, also called Guillaume, stopped Thomas le Blanck on the road, attacked him and demanded money with menaces. Not content with extortion, he then got into a fight in the market place and injured Pierre Verrenck. He, of course, was not found guilty or punished. Guillaume de Tailleur stabbed Jean de Vinceleis and though he was fined, Drogo acted as guarantor which meant that de Tailleur went unpunished. Jean de Barentyn meanwhile locked up several lepers in gaol without permission but, needless to say, he was acquitted.

Guillaume de Tailleur, Guillaume le Warener, Geoffroi Langleis, Henri le Palefraiur and Raoul Turgys, together with Jean de Barentyn, all of whom had been involved in the rapes and gang rapes in the story *A Charge So Horrid*, dragged Jean Dangy of Grouville from his house and set about him leaving him with head injuries, a fractured shin, and wounds to his arms. Jean called the Clameur de Haro (see A Brief history of Jersey, above) and demanded compensation from his attackers. Jean de Barentyn paid a sum of money into the Royal Court and dismissed the offence.

Thomas Malesars and his brother Nicolas somehow managed to offend Drogo de Barentyn. He sent his henchmen to the dwellings of both brothers. Their houses were trashed, their dogs killed and their hens stolen. Both men fled to St Helier and put themselves under the protection of the Bailiff, Jean de Carteret. To no avail. Drogo's henchmen dragged them out and viciously assaulted them. Both of Thomas's arms were broken. Drogo was then called before the Royal Court where he denied everything. Before the case could be tried both brothers withdrew their complaints after intimidation and both were fined for wasting the Court's time.

There were numerous other cases and complaints against Drogo, even that he had his own gallows and prison (the prerogative of the King only), but everyone was in such fear of him and his family that they usually came to nothing. Unbelievably, in 1305, Drogo de Barentyn was appointed Warden of the Isles and in 1309 he was made a Jurat of the Royal Court. Such were the protests about his being Warden of the Isles the King ruled that in future local administrators should not hold this important post. Nevertheless, Drogo held it until 1313 and again in 1315. In 1316, to the immense relief of Jersey, he moved to England. There, despite his long list of crimes, his vicious and unjust behaviour and his inhumane treatment of the islanders, he became Sheriff of Oxfordshire and Berkshire, and keeper of Oxford Castle.

CHAPTER 3

Murder of a Knight
c.1300

The sobbing lady accepted his story as the truth and welcomed him into her home.

This is an early story which did actually happen, though the beginning is more like legend than a foul deed. However, there may be just a bit of allegory which can be simply explained, and the rest is a good old fashioned tale of jealousy, lust and murder. The legend says that once upon a time there was a fearsome dragon who lived in the marshes at St Lawrence and wrought havoc on the countryside. The thing caused so many problems that eventually a deputation was sent to the absentee landlord, Seigneur de Hambye, who lived in Hambye Castle at Paisnel near Coutances in Normandy. The legend goes on to say that the valiant knight and his squire set forth at once on their way to Jersey to sort this creature out.

Later writers point out that the dragon was often a symbol of paganism (non-Christian) in Christian folklore and Christian knights who slew dragons in battle were said to have actually killed pagan chiefs or priests. The most well known of such stories must be that of St George and the Dragon. In fact medieval knights, like the Knights Templar, adopted the cross of St George as their emblem. It is probably reasonably safe to say that some of the earlier pre-Christian cults were still flourishing in remote parts of Jersey and giving the locals, notably local Christians, a hard time of it.

La Hougue Bie, where this story took place, is an impressive passage grave dating from the late Neolithic/Bronze Age. Nearby lie the remains of a tiny village from pre-history. The passage grave has twelve pairs of capstones and a pagan religious ritual area at the far end. The stone entrance is high enough for a small person to stand upright and it is flanked by stone banking among which buzz thousands of tiny bees. The place has undoubtedly been revered ever since it was built and not even the Germans made use of the ready made subterranean structure but built their bunker to the rear of it.

The story goes that the gallant knight attacked the dragon and cut off its head single-handedly (pretty much like St George in fact). It has to be remembered that this all happened during the time of the Knights Templar, a time of intense Christian fervour, and that the good knight was more than likely suppressing the remnants of a pagan cult. However, like his counterpart, St George, he was wounded in the process. After the fight, weak and exhausted, he lay down on the grass, sheltered by a grove of trees, (which evokes strains of Celtic imagery and mythology) to rest and presently fell asleep. The squire, who was envious of the glory that would now be bestowed upon his master and who had, in any case, long fancied his master's wife, saw his opportunity. He drew his sword and killed the Seigneur of Hambye as he slept. Quickly he buried the Seigneur's body in a shallow woodland grave and returned with all speed to Hambye.

The Chatelaine (the Seigneur's lady) had been watching and waiting for her husband's return. Sorrowfully the squire, pretending a grief that he did not feel, told her that a dragon had killed her husband and that he, the squire, had in turn killed the dragon to avenge the Seigneur's death. Finally, he told her that her husband's last wish had been that she should marry the faithful squire so that he could look after her. The sobbing lady accepted his story as the truth and welcomed him into her home. After a decent period of mourning and obedient to what she believed was the Seigneur's dearest wish, the squire and the Chatelaine became man and wife.

The squire, however, who now had everything he had always dreamed of, was still not happy. His conscience was troubling him and he suffered wild nightmares. One night he awoke screaming and drenched in sweat. His wife could not comfort him but held him close as he fell into a fitful sleep. Then he cried out in his sleep that it was he who had murdered his master and he could not bear his burden any longer. The Chatelaine, horrified, yelled for the guards and the squire was thrown into the dungeons until he could be brought to trial. According to the records he finally confessed the truth in the hushed courtroom and was sentenced to death.

La Hougue Bie, showing the quaint and unusual little medieval chapel built above the entrance of the ancient tomb. The author

The Chatelaine was overcome by grief and guilt. Calling her trusted servants, she at once left for Jersey. Before he died the wretched squire had told her where he had buried her husband. She journeyed to the parish of St Saviour and there, on La Hougue Bie, she found the Seigneur's grave. The Chatelaine ordered that a higher mound should be constructed to cover her husband's burial; and then she ordered that a small Christian chapel be built on top of the mound to commemorate forever her husband's Christian beliefs and the triumph of good over evil.

The tiny chapel of Notre Dame de la Clarté (our Lady of the Dawn) on the top of La Hougue Bie dates from the late 1200s. The building of such chapels was a well known method of Christianising pagan sites. The simple stone structure has a small cross over the doorway (which stands directly above the entrance to the pre-historic grave) and inside it is incredibly tranquil, another world away from the hustle of the twenty-first century outside its walls. The brave knight of Hambye seems to have finally found real eternal peace here.

CHAPTER 4

Cry of The Tombelènes
1462

Jeanne gave a piercing shriek which echoed around Le Creux Bouanne. Grabbing the dagger from the Moutonnier she plunged it into his throat ...

On the north-east coast of Trinity parish lies picturesque Bouley Bay. There is a large rock named L'Islet in the middle of the harbour there. One of the best views of the Bay is from the heights of Le Jardin d'Olivet and La Hurette. Stretching along the coast are the precipitous rocky cliffs of the Tombelènes (which take their name from the French and Italian words for falling) in which there is a large cave. Officially it is known as Le Creux Bouanne but for over 500 years, since the following story, it has become known as 'The Place Accursed'.

In 1462, the French raided Jersey, led by the Comte de Maulevrier, and took Mont Orgueil Castle. From there they controlled the eastern part of the island and at night marauding bands of the French raiders would go out sheep stealing. They were known as Les Moutonniers and sometimes as La Ch'valelie because they always rode horseback. Les Moutonniers were feared for their violence and total lack of mercy and Jersey folk learned to dread a knock on the door in the night.

On the western uplands of Bouley in Trinity parish stood a farm called Raulin de l'Ecluse. In the 1460s, when this story takes place, it was still the custom to hold Les Veilles from the first week in September throughout the winter when folks met each night in each other's houses but never two nights following in the same place. They would sit around the fire, telling stories, drinking, singing, sometimes they would dance and maybe the older women

Bouley Bay, c.1936, showing L'Islet (centre) with an incoming tide and the wild cliffs of the Tombelènes. Author's collection

would knit as they sat on the 'jonquière' a 'green bed' made of ferns. It was a pleasant social time for everyone.

The first meeting of Les Veilles was known as L'Assise de Veille and it was turned into a small festival. On that September evening in 1462 L'Assise was held at Raulin de l'Ecluse. It was one of the richer farmsteads and on this night they were also celebrating the engagement of Raulin's son to Jeanne du Jourdain, a local girl. There was a toast to the young couple, a little dancing, a few songs and then folks fell to gossiping. One young man named Pierre said he'd heard that the Moutonniers had been busy over in St Martin the week before. Another called Jean, trying to impress his girl-friend, Néné, said that the Moutonniers didn't scare him and he could take a dozen any time. There was some good natured joshing and then came a knocking at the door. A nervous hush came over the assembly.

Raulin's father hesitantly opened the door. 'Name of a dog, old man! What do you mean by keeping me waiting?' a harsh voice yelled and with these words a Moutonnier burst into the room. Silence fell. The Moutonnier gazed contemptuously around the room then turned on Raulin. 'Leper!' he snarled. 'Do you own this hovel? Then tell this rabble to get down on their knees.' At this point Raulin's son squared his shoulders and hissed 'Get out Norman! Before I pitch you out like a dog!' The Moutonnier hesitated, his hand resting on his dagger. He was outnumbered and he knew it. Backing towards the door he turned towards Raulin's son. 'You will pay dearly for this' he growled. 'I go now but be assured that I shall return and tomorrow you will hang in chains from the castle walls. As for the rest of you . . .' he spat on the floor then turning on his heel he stormed out.

Everyone tried to resume their merry making but the fun had gone out of the evening and soon people started leaving. Raulin's son walked his fiancée back to her cottage. Jeanne was very quiet. 'I am afraid for you, Raulin,' she whispered, 'I have a feeling that something terrible is going to happen. Stay with us tonight.' Raulin smiled indulgently at her. 'You worry needlessly' he said with more reassurance than he felt, but, to keep her happy he agreed that he would take her dog, Fidèle, with him. He could hear thunder in the distance and he knew that a storm was brewing.

As Raulin walked home he thought about his wedding day and how he longed for Jeanne to become his wife; and he did not notice at first that Fidèle was whining uneasily. Then he heard it. The horses hooves galloping towards him. It could only be La Ch'valelie. Raulin knew his main chance of escape lay in flinging himself to the ground behind a bush in the darkness but before he could move a flash of lightening lit the sky behind him and a gruff voice cried 'Qui va la?!' Who goes there? Raulin opened his mouth to reply but a whiplash caught him savagely across the face. Next minute two others of La Ch'valelie brought him crashing to the ground.

Fidèle growled angrily and went to Raulin's defence but one of the Moutonniers whipped out a knife and stabbed at the dog feverishly. Fidèle let out a yelp and limped into the comparative safety of the under-growth. Raulin was bound and gagged and blindfolded before being thrown across the saddle of one of the horses. The Moutonniers rode eastward until they came to Le Creux Bouanne. Here they dismounted and dragged Raulin roughly into the cave.

Jeanne and Raoul with Fidele on the path above the Tombelènes just after their betrothal. Courtesy of the artist, H Niblett

Le Creux Bouanne was well lit with torches stuck in crevices in the cliff and at one end a sheep was roasting over a fire. A large table stood in the centre with mugs of ale upon it and about twenty men sat on rough benches around the table. They stared at Raulin as he was dragged in. Two of his captors cut the thongs that bound his wrists and ankles and hauled him to his feet before leading him to the man who was obviously their chief. To his dismay Raulin saw that it was the Moutonnier who had knocked on his father's door earlier that evening.

'Well!' the man grinned nastily. 'If it isn't the Jersiaise dog who dared to insult me and threatened to throw me out of his home.' He walked around Raulin pushing him this way and that with a contemptuous leer on his face. 'Not quite so brave now,' he said. 'Are we?' Raulin kept quiet with difficulty but he would not give this man the pleasure of a response. 'Too scared to talk, are we, Jersiaise dog?' said the Moutonnier. 'Well I will give you something to think about in your silence. I do not like insolent Jersiaise dogs and I am going to make an example of you. First I am going to have you strung up and then I shall take my dagger and . . .'

'No!' the scream came from the entrance of the cave. Jeanne stood there, the faithful bleeding Fidèle by her side, her eyes blazing with defiance. 'Raulin,' she said, 'I have come to plead for your life but if they kill you I will die with you for I do not want to live without you.' The Moutonnier chief was impressed by Jeanne's courage as she stepped forward and stood between Raulin and his tormentors but he would not let a mere chit of a girl sway him. Roughly, he grabbed her and dragged her to him. Raulin, incensed, lunged at the Moutonnier, but the Moutonnier swiftly pulled out his dagger and stabbed Raulin through the heart. Giving a single cry Raulin fell dead at Jeanne's feet.

Jeanne gave a piercing shriek which echoed around Le Creux Bouanne. Grabbing the dagger from the Moutonnier she plunged it into his throat, then she ran screaming from the cave. The storm was still raging as the Moutonniers gave chase. The anguished screaming could still be heard then a flash of lightening lit the sky and Jeanne could be seen on the rock of L'Islet, her arms outstretched, her hair blowing in the wind. As the tide came in she let the sea take her and she never ceased her unearthly screaming until her head disappeared beneath the waves.

A week later her body was washed up near the cave and she was buried with her beloved Raulin in the little churchyard of Trinity

Parish Church. They would lie together forever, gone but not forgotten. Jeanne's frantic screaming is still said to be heard on stormy nights and it has become known as the Cry of the Tombelènes; and since that time too Le Creux Bouanne has been known as The Place Accursed. Adding to this reputation is the legend of '. . . a huge black dog with saucer eyes . . .' which is said to have haunted Bouley Bay for centuries. There is an inn overlooking the Bay named after the dog and the usual tales concerning the appearance of a black dog are whispered around local firesides. The dog is said to be the devil in disguise, a harbinger of death and destruction which will bring disaster to all those unlucky enough to see it, huge eyes luminous in the darkness.

Today, the reality of Bouley Bay is sometimes hard to reconcile with its legends of dark deeds and devilish dogs. The bay has a wide sandy beach and Jersey Divers have their headquarters there. The name of the Tombelènes is no longer used, although the area can be traced through old maps and documents. Nevertheless, the cliffs and caves of the Trinity Parish coastline are clearly visible and so is the little rocky outcrop of L'Islet from which Jeanne hurled herself on that stormy night in 1462. Any romantic or tragic ambience however is brought firmly down to earth by Mad Mary's Kiosk, just a stone's throw from L'Islet, which sells that delightful modern duet of hot steaming tea together with marmite and toast. Yet when the people have gone and the sky is darkening and the wind is getting up it is still just possible to hear the echoes of the Cry of the Tombelènes.

CHAPTER 5

Trial by Battle
1494

This in itself would have been a remarkable enough journey for any woman on her own ... Margaret de Carteret made it only days after having giving birth to her twenty-first child.

The de Carteret family and St Ouen are virtually synonymous, the family having been resident there since the days of William the Conqueror and having provided the Seigneurs of the parish since King John's time. Although this story centres around Philippe de Carteret, the real heroine is his wife, Margaret, a woman of daring, courage, determination and immense physical stamina. Her father, Sir Richard Harliston, together with Sir Philippe de Carteret, had been instrumental in recovering Mont Orgueil and its port in the Wars of the Roses under Edward IV. Subsequently, Sir Philippe's son, also called Philippe, had married Sir Richard's daughter, Margaret.

Margaret knew that her main role in life was to provide sons for her husband. She did not complain. She was healthy and she loved children, but secretly she wanted a daughter; another female in the family to whom she could talk and with whom she could share empathy. After she had given birth to half a dozen fine strapping boys her husband had no objection to her wanting a daughter. He had his sons and if a daughter would make her happy then so be it. However, the boys just kept on coming. After giving birth to twenty children, all of whom were sons, a lesser woman might have given up but Margaret was determined. Just one daughter, she prayed, just one, whatever it took, and she would be happy. Her wish was finally granted when, after her twenty-first pregnancy, she at last gave birth to a baby girl. She gazed, adoring and unbelieving, at her new daughter as the baby lay in her cradle.

Whatever it took, and it had taken giving birth to twenty boys first, Margaret didn't mind. She was proud of her sons and now at last she had her reward. A daughter. Her very own little girl.

Margaret's joy in her new baby was soon marred however by what was happening to her husband. Philippe de Carteret had been brave, rash or foolish enough to accuse the English Governor of Jersey of 'abuse of privilege'. The Governor retaliated with a forged letter which suggested that de Carteret had been going to betray the Castle of Gorey to the French. Philippe de Carteret hotly protested his innocence, slandering the Governor liberally in the process until one of the Governor's 'strong men' challenged him to a duel. He accepted this challenge with alacrity, relishing the chance to prove the Governor a liar and a coward.

The terms laid down were that until the day of the duel both men were to be kept in Gorey Castle. Unknown to de Carteret, however, the henchman was being fed like a king while de Carteret was given only bread and water. The Governor had also forbidden any boats to leave Jersey for England. He did not wish Henry VII to discover what he was doing to Jersey's 'premier Seigneur' until he'd had a chance to explain matters to the King himself. However, when Margaret took the new baby to meet her father she was shocked by the state in which she found her husband and she knew at once that he would be no match for the Governor's man. Furthermore, she realised that her only hope lay in appealing to the King directly and telling him the truth; but how could she do that when all direct contact with the mainland was cut off from the island.

Margaret was a resourceful woman and she thought about the problem carefully before laying her plans. She asked a fisherman to take her to Guernsey so that she would not be seen to be contravening the Governor's orders; from Guernsey she sailed to Poole in a cutter, a small but fast sailing ship, which covered the distance swiftly. As soon as she arrived in Poole she rode by coach and four across the rough countryside roads to Sheen where the King had his Court. This in itself would have been a remarkable enough journey for any woman on her own to make in the late fifteenth century but Margaret de Carteret made it only days after having giving birth to her twenty-first child and she'd had to leave her adored new daughter behind on Jersey.

King Henry VII was impressed both by Margaret's courage and by her maternal achievements. He listened to her story carefully

Gorey in the late nineteenth century, with Mont Orgueil Castle in the background. The railway no longer exists. Author's collection

and then he agreed that her husband should be tried by the English Privy Council instead of the Jersey courts. Margaret received her precious letter with the King's commands and the Royal Seal and then she rode at full speed to Southampton. Although exhausted she did not rest but took a boat for Jersey and landed back on the island the night before the duel was due to take place. Triumphantly, she rode straight to Gorey castle and handed the King's letter to the Governor. The Governor was furious but even he did not dare to disobey his King. Philippe de Carteret was released and sent to England for trial where he was duly acquitted. Margaret de Carteret became a folk heroine for the way in which she had saved her husband's life as well as for the number of young de Carteret men to whom she had given birth.

CHAPTER 6

Bewitching Jersey
1500–1700

Something as simple as a mole or a birthmark ... was enough to condemn a person to being tied up and roasted until there was nothing but a pile of ashes left.

The later Middle Ages leading up to the Renaissance of the 1500s and 1600s was a period fraught with superstition, genius, creativity, fear and a widespread obsession with witchcraft. While Leonardo da Vinci was painting his masterpieces and inventing submarine and aircraft centuries ahead of his time, and Shakespeare was writing his enduring plays, women (mostly) and a few men were dying in screaming agony, tortured and burned alive at the stake for reasons which don't even merit the description of significant, let alone justified. Something as simple as a mole or a birthmark or just a simple blemish of the skin, which even today most of the population still have in some form somewhere on their bodies, was enough to condemn a person to being tied up and roasted until there was nothing but a pile of ashes left.

The parish of St Clements seems to have been regarded as the 'witching parish'. The local witch 'headquarters' was said to be at Rocqberg, known locally as The Witches Rocks. These rocks stand on what is now strictly private property and can only be seen from a distance of several yards away behind tall closed iron gates. Overshadowed by trees, the rock formation appears to consist of three parts and a small water waterfall tumbles down them. It is hard to ascertain from a distance whether this is a natural or man-made feature. A faint smell, suspiciously like incense, pervades the air, giving a distinctly eerie feel to the whole place. Nearby, the sinister looking Green Island and La Rocq Harbour, with its stark

La Rocq Tower standing on the outer reefs of the bay, add to the general feeling of other-worldness.

St Clements is very different from the other parishes of Jersey. More remote than the others, even today, it is quiet and full of the past with its wild drowning coastline, creeper covered ruins, ancient church and the fourteenth century Longueville Manor, now a five star hotel although no one appears to have told its resident ghost that times have changed. Victor Hugo lived on the Grève d'Azette in St Clements for three years and while there he claimed to have had visions of God and conversations with Christ.

Two of the most popular 'tests of witchcraft' were the Catch 22 witches mark and water tests. Witches were supposed to have a distinguishing mark so an inquisitor (almost always a man) would conduct a diligent search of the body of the alleged witch (almost always a woman) until a spot on the skin was found which appeared insensible to pain and did not bleed when pricked. This is a task which any reasonably efficient acupuncturist should be able to carry out. The modern mindset does not need a degree in rocket science to suspect that there were either sexual or sado-masochistic elements involved here. When such a spot was found and it did not bleed then the accused was guilty. If it did bleed s/he was sent back to prison for further 'interrogation' which usually meant torture. For the water test the alleged witch was thrown into a river or lake. If they floated they were guilty. If they sank they were innocent but usually drowned. Hence these tests were very much a 'no-win' situation for the accused.

Witch hysteria was such that even Jeanne d'Arc, who saved her country for the rather incompetent Dauphin of the time after receiving a very Christian religious vision, was denounced as a witch by a French ecclesiastical court. She was found guilty of heresy and sorcery and handed over to the English who obligingly had her burned at the stake in the market place of Rouen on 30 May 1431. Jersey had fewer prosecutions for witchcraft than neighbouring Guernsey but the practice was still very prevalent; so much so that the Royal Court passed an Act at the end of the sixteenth century denouncing 'diabolical practices . . .' and also declared that those involved in meting out justice should cease seeking assistance or herbal remedies for their physical ailments from so-called witches in order '. . . that Divine vengeance may be averted. . .' In October 1591, Matthew Le Brocq and John Le Brocq, who sought a herbal cure from a witch for John's daughter, were '... ordered to the Castle ...' A comparatively minor fate befell Jean Bichard who obtained herbal remedies to heal a leg wound. He was made to do penance in the parish stocks of St Peter on 1 July 1595.

Jersey is said to have prohibited the actual use of torture on witches. While on Guernsey witches were burned alive, on Jersey they were strangled first. An unpleasant form of death but better than the flames. On 5 November 1585, Jean Mourant, 'fils Philippe' (and one of the few men convicted of witchcraft), was '... condemned to be strangled until he is dead ... [and] to have his body burnt until it is entirely consumed ...' In 1562, a witch named only as Anne, who came from St Brelade, was strangled and burned for witchcraft in St Helier and Michelle La Blanche was hanged at Les Hurets in St Ouen. Marie Filleul of St Clement suffered the same fate in 1623 when she was hanged on the Seigneur's gallows at Samares Manor. Marie Esnouf followed suit on 1 June 1648; followed two weeks later on 15 June by Marie Grandin of St Ouen. Marie Esnouf, a vicar's granddaughter, was condemned because she had a 'black mark upon her palate and ... when pierced with a lancet, she felt no pain ...' Marie Grandin died because she had her head shaved and a mark was found on her skull. One side bled but the other did not. St Clement, the tiniest parish, seemed to be regarded as the 'centre' of island witchcraft. Five witches from there were executed: Jean Mourant, Collette Horman, Ysic Hardyne and Germaine Royal in 1611; and Marie Filleul.

A note of sanity and sad reflection was finally introduced by the Lieutenant Bailiff, Philip Le Geyt, who held office from 1676-1715. He wrote:

> ... as Holy Scripture forbids us to allow witches to live, many persons have made it a matter of conscience and religion to be severe in respect of such a crime. This principle has without doubt made many persons credulous. How often have purely accidental associations been taken as convincing proofs? How many innocent people have perished in the flames on the asserted testimony of supernatural evidence? I will not say there are no witches; but ever since the difficulty of convicting them has been recognised in the island, they all seem to have disappeared, as though the evidence of times gone by had been but an illusion. This shows the instability of all things here below ...

CHAPTER 7

The Soldier's Love
1523

... he talked to Marguerite as the sons of the Serpent speak to the daughters of Eve ...

Even by Tudor times the de Carterets had been Seigneurs (Squires) of St Ouens for centuries and they held large estates within the parish. During the early years of the 1500s one of their manor farms was tenanted by a former sailor who had returned to his homeland after spending several years at sea. By the time this story takes place he had two grown up sons to help him farm the land and a daughter named Marguerite who kept house for him. Sadly, his wife was now an invalid, who was both blind and deaf, but Marguerite cared for her mother as she cooked and cleaned and washed for her father and brothers. It was a hard and often lonely life for the girl but she did not complain.

In 1523, Marguerite celebrated her sixteenth birthday. Her father was on good terms with the Seigneur, Helier de Carteret, and her godmother was one of the de Carteret ladies from the Manor. Marguerite was a lithe attractive girl with brown eyes and dark hair but she was not what would be described today as 'street-wise'. She had a rather innocent trusting nature and was in some ways very naïve; a combination which was to prove both tragic and fatal.

One morning soon after her sixteenth birthday she was pegging out the washing when a voice called to her. Turning round she saw one of the soldiers from Mont Orgueil Castle. Shyly she said, 'Hello.' The soldier smiled. He was riding a splendid horse and was, he told her, returning to the castle from a hunting expedition. They spoke for a few moments and the soldier, or 'gallant' as soldiers were then termed for the brave deeds of protection which they were supposed to undertake, was much taken with the pretty country girl. He resolved to see her again and told her that he would call on her soon.

A few days later the soldier came to the cottage as Marguerite was at work and asked if he might come in and talk to her. They sat side by side on the 'jonquière', the soft green bed of ferns which each Jersey cottage had by its fireside, and he told her softly that he had loved her from the moment he had first set eyes on her and that she was constantly in his thoughts. He took her hands and gazed deep into her eyes as he spoke these words and Marguerite was lost. Her father and brothers were out working in the fields and her mother lay ill in bed upstairs unable to either see or hear what was happening. The soldier painted a rosy picture of their future together as he took Marguerite in his arms and kissed her; and she did not resist when his hands slid gently under her skirt.

It was of course the oldest story in the world. Once the soldier had 'had his way with her' Marguerite did not see her 'gallant' again. Furthermore, after a few weeks, the girl realised that she was pregnant and the enormity of her situation began to dawn upon her. She tried to hide her condition but, alone during the day, she wept hot tears of shame and despair. Her mother sensed the change in her daughter and tried to comfort her. One day as she held Marguerite close to her she felt the rounded bump of Marguerite's belly and realised suddenly the reason for her daughter's distress. The shock of this discovery killed her.

Full of guilt and grief, Marguerite now confessed everything to her father and brothers. They were furious and her two brothers left immediately for Mont Orgueil Castle to find the 'gallant' responsible for their sister's condition. Upon their arrival they demanded to see the Governor, Sir Henry Vaughan. However, when they poured out their tale of woe Vaughan just laughed. Turning to a soldier standing beside him he said, 'Well, nephew, what is my niece going to say about this?' The soldier blushed violently, for he had recently married the Governor's niece, and denied everything, calling Marguerite's brothers a pair of worthless liars. This was too much and the elder brother punched the soldier in the face, leaving him bloodied and bruised. As a result both the brothers were arrested and imprisoned in the castle's dungeons.

When his sons did not return home, Marguerite's father feared the worst. Dressing himself in his best clothes he spoke more kindly to his weeping daughter than he had done for several days and bade her look after the house while he was away. Then he set

out for Mont Orgueil Castle. Ordinarily he would have appealed to
the Seigneur but Helier de Carteret was away in London defending
himself on charges laid against him by Sir Henry Vaughan. However, as Marguerite's father had known Vaughan in his seafaring
days he hoped to be able to appeal to the man's better nature.

Vaughan listened carefully and sympathetically to the old man's
tale. At first he offered money but this was refused. Marguerite's
father wanted to challenge the Governor's nephew-in-law to a
duel. Vaughan, who had daughters of his own, finally agreed to
this request. It was however an unequal contest and Marguerite's
father was soon killed by the 'gallant'. Her brothers remained in
prison and so it was a few days before Marguerite learned what had
happened. Her neighbours had little sympathy for Marguerite's
plight and hurled abuse at her, leaving the poor girl in wretched
and tearful despair. Eventually, as Marguerite wondered what on
earth was to become of her, the sister of the curate at St Ouen's
Parish Church took her in and gave her food, shelter and warmth
and showed her some humanity and kindness; and it was here that
Marguerite's baby was born.

Marguerite took a few days to recover from giving birth. Then,
swaddling her baby carefully and dressing herself in deepest
mourning, Marguerite took to presenting herself before the 'gallant' whenever he went out and about, begging alms for her child.
The soldier's wife became curious about this strange creature forever holding out a baby towards her husband and asked who she
was. On learning the truth she became very upset and threatened
her husband that if he ever saw Marguerite again she would return
to her parents in England and tell her father that her marriage had
been built on lies and was therefore false.

By now the 'gallant' was becoming very anxious. He enjoyed a
comfortable and affluent lifestyle married to the Governor's niece
and he did not want to give that up. Desperately, he begged
Vaughan to exile Marguerite from Jersey. Vaughan refused.
Marguerite had committed no crime and privately Vaughan considered his nephew-in-law's punishment rather apt. Finally, the
soldier devised a plan to rid himself of Marguerite and her un-
wanted attentions.

Marguerite was overjoyed when her soldier lover rode over to
see her one fine morning. He had, he told her, been neglecting her
of late, for which he was sorry. However, he had bought some
presents for the child and he suggested that he should take her and

Grève De Lecq, the lonely bay from where Marguerite was rowed to her death.
Author's collection

the baby out on a picnic. Eagerly, she dressed herself in her best frock and, carrying the baby in her arms, walked with her lover along the quiet sunlit lanes to Grève de Lecq where the soldier said he had procured a rowing boat for their outing. He helped her and the child into the boat and set out to row around Plémont Point to what was known as the Big Cave. Drawing the boat up onto the sands the 'gallant' left them there telling Marguerite that he was going to fetch the food for their picnic. She watched him clamber up the steep rocks to the top of the cliffs and then she took her baby into the entrance of the cave to await his return.

The roar of the sea awoke Marguerite from her dreams of becoming the soldier's wife. She did not know how long she had been there but the soldier seemed to have been gone for ages. As she got to her feet she saw to her horror that the rapidly incoming tide had cut her off. The wind had risen and the waves were rough. Marguerite clutched her baby to her and wondered desperately what she should do. The little rowing boat was still there, bobbing up and down on the tide, so, hitching up her skirts,

12. NEEDLE ROCK, PELMONT, JERSEY.

The cave where Marguerite and her baby were left to drown. Author's collection

Marguerite waded out to it. Placing her baby in the bottom of the boat, she clambered in over the side and began to row. The current here however was strong and treacherous and despite her best efforts the little boat was continually dashed against the rocks. She screamed desperately for help as she tried to row herself and her child to safety but there was no one to hear. No one that is except for the 'gallant' who sat quietly up on the cliffs watching Marguerite's struggles. Finally one wave, larger than the rest, lifted the little boat out of the water and dropped it onto the dark deadly rocks below. Marguerite and her baby were flung into the sea and quickly disappeared beneath the foaming waters. Only now did the 'gallant' act and began scrambling down the cliffs to make some sort of belated, half-hearted rescue attempt. It was of course too late. Marguerite and her child were drowned and their bodies were washed ashore the next morning.

Soon afterwards, Helier de Carteret, who was also the Bailiff of Jersey, returned to the island in triumph, having won his law suit against Vaughan. He was furious when he heard the story of Marguerite's seduction, her tragic ending, her brother's imprisonment and her father's death. His sister's goddaughter had deserved better than this. Vaughan was recalled to England and Marguerite's brothers were released. Then de Carteret put the 'gallant' on trial. Had Marguerite's soldier lover been of lowly birth he would have been executed almost at once. However, he had been well enough connected to marry the niece of the Governor and it was generally felt that a brief dalliance with a country girl which had gone wrong was hardly cause enough to send a man of noble birth to the gallows. As it was he was simply ordered to pay a sum of compensation to Marguerite's brothers for the death of their sister and her child. It was a sad ending to a tragic tale.

CHAPTER 8

The Spanish Ships
c.1530

... a wave larger than the rest swept the young girl into the sea ... dashing her against the rocks beneath the swirling waters ...

Wrecking is a cruel sport but there have always been wreckers; people whose own selfish greed outweighs any concern for their fellow beings. It is even worse when the wreckers themselves are sea-faring folk (and they usually are) who know just how phenomenally powerful and pitiless the sea can be. Wrecking a ship is not a casual robbery like someone running off with a purse or stealing food because they are hungry. The victims of wreckers almost invariably end up in a watery grave and this puts wrecking, by definition a pre-meditated crime, out of the category of robbery and firmly into the category of murder. For this reason the following story may be seen as a tale of poetic justice.

In 1492 Columbus had begun the colonisation of North America (the discovery of the continent belonged to another explorer, Amerigo Vespucci, hence the name of America) and in the years following the Conquistadores began the conquest and subjugation of South America. As a result Spain's empire grew to be the largest and richest in the world. Huge Spanish galleons full of treasure regularly made the trip home across the Atlantic. In particular the Aztec and Inca civilisations of South America were heavily plundered. The South American natives despised the Spanish greed for gold but gave it to them in the hope that the Conquistadores would go away if they had got what they came to get. It was a vain hope and the destruction of the native South American civilisations is a stain on the history of Spain. However, in all fairness to the Spaniards, they were not the only ones greedy for gold.

Fleets of treasure ships made the hazardous crossing from South America to Spain two or three times a year, laden with gold, bringing undreamed of wealth back to their mother country. One dark night during the late autumn of 1495 a great storm arose, smashing its fury over the Channel Islands. The wind howled and lashed rain against the cabins and the rigging of the fleet of ships making its uncertain way across the Channel towards the coast of the Continent. The ships lurched and teetered and lurched again, large ungainly galleons which were no match for the furious waves crashing over their decks. These were the days of sail when there were no handy engines to get a ship out of trouble if the wind veered in the wrong direction. Caught by the storm five of the great Spanish treasure ships were being driven relentlessly towards the treacherous rocks of the Jersey coast. They had not gone un-noticed. On the desolate uplands of Le Grande Cueillete a group of men assembled at Les Hasnières to watch the plight of the big ships, their torn sails flapping in the wind as they drifted helplessly towards the land.

The men made no attempts at helping the great vessels in their struggles for they had recognised what they were. They simply waited for the ships to strike the rocks and then they would go on a pillaging trip which would bring them untold fortunes. There was however a lull in the storm and this gave the Spanish sailors a temporary advantage. With difficulty they managed to turn their ships about and began to head once again for the open sea. The would be wreckers watched in stunned disbelief and then they went into rapid action. Hurrying to the most exposed and rocky part of the coast they quickly built a few small bonfires and lit them as beacons to lure the ships back into shore.

The Spanish sailors, on seeing the lights, turned their ships around again and began to head towards them thinking the beacons a guide to safe harbour where they could ride out the storm at anchor. Too late, they realised their mistake as the vicious and jagged teeth of the rocks loomed menacingly out of the water. Four of the ships struck and sank immediately with all hands. No matter, the wreckers knew that the cargoes would eventually wash ashore. The fifth and largest ship swept in towards the shore and eventually became trapped fast in a gully between the rocks. The seas washed angrily over her decks to which an old man and a young girl clung desperately. On seeing the men on the shore the old man implored them to save his daughter. Knowing it would be

Spanish ships sunk by wreckers near La Corbiere. Courtesy of the artist, H Niblett

best that no one should survive to tell the tale, the wreckers ignored his pleas and turned away impassively. At that moment a wave larger than the rest swept the young girl into the sea and dragged her down to her death, dashing her against the rocks beneath the swirling waters. Her father watched in shocked and tragic disbelief then he turned on the wreckers and cursed them.

'You may have my gold' he screamed at them above the noise of the storm, 'but you have taken my daughter and now you are your-selves condemned to die the same cruel death. You will see. Within the year I will meet you beneath the waters of this bay!' At this there was a groaning of timbers and splintering of wood and then the great ship sank slowly beneath the waves, taking the old man with it.

If the wreckers felt a moment's unease it was soon dispelled as treasure chests floated to the surface. Eagerly they began to drag them ashore. Prising open the lids they were stunned by the quantity and quality of the gold. Now they would indeed be rich men. Dragging home their prizes the wreckers happily planned what they would do with all this unexpected wealth, and for the next twelve months they lived like lords in the most sumptuous luxury, but as the anniversary of the sinking drew near there was a feeling of apprehension in the air. The leader of the band of wreckers decided to brazen it out by holding a feast for his followers. Much wine and brandy was drunk and then the leader rose to his feet for a toast, 'Death by this liquor if death it be, for no drop of water will henceforth pass my lips!'

The light in the crasset flickered and then there was an almighty crash of thunder. In the dusk, their senses dulled by drink, none of them had noticed the approaching storm. Lightening flashed, there was another clap of thunder and then the heavens opened, deluging them with such torrential rain as they had never known. As they ran for the shelter of their squat fishermen's cottages they heard a roar that seemed to come straight from the depths of Neptune's belly. The next moment the wind was upon them, uprooting trees, wrecking cottages and whirling the unfortunate wreckers along in its path, tossing them this way and that like autumn leaves.

For years afterwards Jersey people spoke in hushed and frightened tones of the magic wind that had come from nowhere, sweeping the drunken revellers into the sea, and covering their lands with blown sand. To this day huge sand dunes stretch across La Moye Common towards La Quennevais, where the wreckers had lived. It seemed that the old man's desperate curse had come true. Superstition was, and is, strong on Jersey, so, although there was a very possible natural explanation, the legend has grown up. Strong to hurricane force winds are not unknown in advance of a storm, nor are the 'twisters' (tornadoes) or waterspouts they bring in their wake. The truly uncanny part is the timing, 25 November, exactly a year to the day after the wreckers had sent the unfortunate Spanish mariners to their death; but then truth is often stranger than fiction.

Chapter 9

The Mardi Gras Wedding
1540

He threw the hapless old man into a cold empty room ... then sought out the ravishing Mrs Sarre and spent the rest of the night with her.

Michael Sarre should have been able to count himself fortunate. He was the richest man on Jersey, he lived in a fine house named La Maison de St Jean near St Ouen's Manor, and he was married to a beautiful young woman. His problem was that he was no longer in the first flush of youth. To put it more bluntly, he was old and he was tired and he had a sneaking feeling that his young wife thought so too. There were, he knew, plenty of young and not so young men who had cast covetous eyes upon her. One of them was Edward de Carteret, aged twenty-two, the illegitimate son of one of the oldest, if not one of the most popular, families on the island.

Edward de Carteret was a man used to getting what he wanted and what he wanted was young Mrs Sarre, not to mention the huge fortune she would have if only her useless old fool of a husband would die. Michael Sarre might have been elderly but he seemed to be in good health and, thought de Carteret sourly, was just obstinate enough to live to a good ripe old age, if only to spite him and prevent the hapless Mrs Sarre from having any fun before she herself was too old. In the end, de Carteret, consumed with envy and lust, decided to give fate a helping hand.

One cold winter's night he rode stealthily up to La Maison de St Jean and broke into the house. Pulling his cloak tightly around him to obscure his identity, Edward de Carteret sought out the old man's bedroom. He smiled grimly to himself when he found it. Closing the door softly, de Carteret viciously dragged Michael Sarre from his bed and brutally attacked him, injuring him grievously. He threw the hapless old man into a cold empty room and fastened the door with a rope so that Sarre could not escape to summon help. Then de Carteret sought out the ravishing Mrs Sarre and spent the rest of the night with her. In all fairness she may well not have known what he had done to her husband as it was the custom then for those couples who could afford it to have separate bedrooms; this being seen as a sign of class and breeding.

Michael Sarre was left locked in the cold empty room, alone and untended, badly hurt, and without warmth, food or medical attention. It did not take long for him to die of his injuries. Edward de Carteret feigned great surprise upon the discovery of the body and it was assumed that Sarre had disturbed intruders who had beaten him senseless and then locked him up so that they could make their getaway. His widow appeared to grieve but, two weeks after his funeral, on Shrove Tuesday, the day of the Mardi Gras, she secretly married Edward de Carteret in a romantic ceremony amidst the ruins of the thirteenth century Chapel of St Marie de Lec. The small stone-built chapel stood just to the north of St Ouen's Manor overlooking the wild and beautiful coast of Grève de Lecq. A Catholic priest, known as Philippe L'Hermit, lived among the chapel ruins and he agreed to conduct the clandestine wedding ceremony. There were no wedding guests and John Leland wrote in his *Itinerary* that it was the 'final appearance in history' of the little chapel.

De Carteret now had everything he'd wanted: pretty wife, grand house, large fortune; but the tongues had started to wag and the local magistrates were far from satisfied with the accounts given of how Michael Sarre had come to meet his death. Further enquiries were made and searching questions were asked. Finally, Edward de Carteret was apprehended and taken before the Royal Court. He tried to bluster and bluff his way out of the situation, protesting his innocence, but his accusers were not convinced. The Court however deemed de Carteret's crime much too serious to be heard on Jersey and, most unusually, he was tried before the Star Chamber, a court noted for neither its mercy nor its humanity. The verdict, frustratingly, was not recorded, or at least has not survived, but almost certainly Edward de Carteret would have been condemned to pay the supreme penalty for such a heinous crime.

Chapter 10

The House of Death
1600s

... inside, the house was completely covered in blood ...

The parish of St Brelade seems to have attracted perhaps rather more than its fair share of tragedy. The setting for this story is the small pretty town of St Aubin. The town was named after the Bishop of Angers who did much to protect the island from pirates; although, ironically it became a centre for the privateers who were little other than legalized pirates. During the seventeenth and eighteenth centuries St Aubin was the main port of Jersey although today it is probably better known for the Old Court House which appeared as a pub in the well known television series *Bergerac*. One of the town's other claims to fame is the Royal Channel Islands Yacht Club on the quay whose first woman member was the actress Lily Langtry known as 'The Jersey Lily' because of her beauty.

During the seventeenth century the little port of St Aubin became a centre for thousands of French Protestants fleeing from religious persecution by their Catholic counterparts in France. Jersey had been fiercely Protestant since Edward Seymour's reign as Governor in the mid 1500s. Many of the Huguenots were skilled craftsmen and textile workers. They were welcomed in Jersey which had a booming and lucrative cottage industry in knitting woollen stockings. So much so that in 1608 an Act was passed forbidding knitting during the harvest period because there were not enough people to work the land and gather in the crops.

Life should have been good for the inhabitants of St Aubins at this time but some of them suffered a complete and utter nightmare. It was the screaming which terrified them so much. On an island where people could be publicly flogged almost to death and witches were burned at the stake they should have been used to inhuman screams of pain and rage and despair, but these screams were even worse. They came from one house in the back streets of St Aubin. Yet no one dared to investigate their cause because if St Aubin folk were terrified of the screams they were even more terrified of the owner of this particular house and even their sense of public duty and compassion could not overcome their fear.

In St Aubin there were several houses which took in refugees and the owner of one of them seemed particularly friendly as he greeted each new batch of arrivals at the quay. He invited them to stay with him while they got their bearings in their new land and found themselves work and lodgings. If it was noticed that he was perhaps interested in the more affluent refugees no one said anything. They went gratefully enough with him to his home where they were given a good meal and a bed for the night. Then the darkness came. The innocent trusting refugees who had gone with this man were terrorised and subjected to an ordeal of violence and death which plumbed the Satanic depths. The screaming

St Aubin town c.1900, featured in the detective series Bergerac *and town of the* House of Death. Author's collection

lasted most of the night, night after night. The neighbourhood was petrified by the screams and groans and shrieks which came from this house in the middle of the night. It seems inconceivable that no-one had the courage to investigate or to take action but locals were absolutely terrified of the owner of the house and feared what he might do to them and their children if they breathed a word.

However, after one particularly dreadful night of incessant screaming and shrieks of pain, a few of the braver ones somehow finally plucked up sufficient courage and went to investigate. The sight which greeted them was absolutely horrifying. Inside the house was completely covered in blood although someone had made an unsuccessful attempt to scrub the bloodstains from the walls and floors. Gouges could be seen in the plaster where some-one had desperately tried to claw their way out of this hell by their fingernails. It was quite literally a bloodbath. Worst of all in the garden were a number of freshly dug shallow graves where the mutilated remains of the hapless victims had been buried after being savagely murdered and robbed of their money and valuables.

The owner of the house, a callous and heartless murderer, was swiftly apprehended and brought to trial. It was a short trial for it is impossible to think that there could be any defence for the crimes that had been perpetrated. The details were so dreadful that they were not made public and not long afterwards the unnamed murderer paid the supreme penalty for his crimes. There was however no peace for the residents of St Aubin. The shrieks and screams continued to be heard in what had become known as The House of Death. Eventually the situation became so bad that the authorities were forced to demolish the place and this finally put an end to the noises if not to the gruesome memories.

CHAPTER 11

Smuggling Misdeeds in Les Ecréhous and Jersey 1600s–1800s

When they were recovered the female bodies were found to have £1,000 worth of silks wrapped around them under their ordinary clothes.

Islands are good smuggling country. They are also often a 'back door' into certain countries for the revenue men do not have the manpower or resources for customs posts in every possible place where contraband might be brought ashore. For the authorities there is also the difficulty of policing coastlines which are usually remote, often treacherous, and offer a multitude of possible hiding places. For the smugglers these same coastlines offer multiple opportunities for concealing smuggled goods such as caves or nicely hidden locations where smuggling 'cachés' can be built and perhaps reached by underground tunnels from the landing places.

Jersey was no exception to the rule. By 1689, there was an 'immense smuggling trade' between England and France. There are a number of Creux on all of the island's coasts with names like The Pirate's Cave, Le Creux au Musc, Smuggler's Caves, La Cave ès Fraudeurs, Le Creux du Vis (The Devil's Hole origins Scandinavian 'vic' meaning a creek). Also known as Les Creux des Fées are the Creux Fantômes at St Brelade and there a number of deep indentations or crevices in the cliffs some of which are reminiscent in shape of fairies, ghost and phantoms. The spooky reputations of these caves did the smuggling trade no harm for it meant that most folk would keep their distance after nightfall. Jersey is, and was, full of lonely stretches of coastline which made ideal smuggling haunts; such as Portelet, where there is still an old

et at Corbiere, Jersey.

Corbière Rocks and Lightouse, a wreckers' paradise. Author's collection

smuggler's inn high above the Côte Brelade that was home to Western Europe's oldest known human settlement: La Quennais, opposite La Corbière Lighthouse, where wreckers use to lure ships on to the treacherous rocks; the wild and merciless cliffs around Bouley Bay and The Tombelènes; and the small remote isles and islets of Les Ecréhous with their vicious protecting reefs.

There are five islands in Les Ecréhous big enough upon which to actually build a house. Le Maître Île (the Master Isle) is the largest. At the southern end are the ruins of a small chapel and a medieval priory founded in 1203; and the island has a number of huts (as the habitational dwellings are called) dating from the prehistoric to the present. La Marmotière has about twenty huts, mostly nineteenth century. La Blianque Île (White Island) had four huts on a central shingle spit. These were washed away in 1912 and three modern huts have been built on higher ground. La Grande Brecque and La Petite Brecque boast just one hut each and at times of the high spring tides any inhabitants make for one of the other islands to keep themselves and their possessions dry and above water.

At low water these tiny islands appear to be joined by a winding causeway and there is evidence to suggest that until the mid 1700s Les Ecréhous may have been a single island. During the eighteenth and nineteenth centuries quarrying was officially recorded as the major industry but this unlikely setting was actually a major centre of smuggling for over 300 years, from the mid 1500s to the late 1800s. As Les Ecréhous are officially part of Jersey, access was not restricted to Channel Islanders. However, the islands were considered too small to have a customs post and as they are barely a dozen miles from France their situation was considered ideal for smuggling.

During the 1690s the chief commodities smuggled through Les Ecréhous were lead and powder which were sent on to St Malo for use as ammunition. This trade reached such proportions that a complaint was made to the Council of State which resulted in a request to the Lieutenant-Governor, Edward Harris, to halt the ammunitions trade. However, this proved to be a tad awkward because the Lieutenant-Governor was himself one of the smugglers!

Later, tobacco and brandy became the most popular contraband items. In 1881, a very zealous Impôt agent (French Customs officer) named H C Bertram impounded the *Kosma*, captained by Polydore Binet, on Les Ecréhous. He ordered the boat towed to Gorey on Saturday evening but he did not inspect the cargo until the Monday morning. All the barrels proved to be full of nothing more than water and Bertram was reprimanded by his employers for making them look fools. After that episode he became increasing eccentric and took to stalking Les Ecréhous as though he personally owned them.

The levels of smuggling activity on Les Ecréhous in the eighteenth and nineteenth centuries is evidenced by the number of good quality pottery finds and the large quantities of old wine bottles discovered in the rubbish middens of the islands. Les Ecréhous were also popular for vote rigging during this period. Opposition voters to a favoured candidate in important local elections often found themselves spending a night on the islands, having been taken there and dumped until the elections were over.

On the 'mainland', as those on Les Ecréhous referred to Jersey, the most commonly smuggled goods included tea, tobacco and brandy. In the 1820s, before the introduction of French tea, the import tax on tea had risen to 96 per cent and such high import taxes made smuggling of tea inevitable. Jean Martel (1684–1753), a Jerseyman whose name is synonymous with brandy, emigrated to France and in 1715 he founded a trading house in Cognac and began exporting the fine brandy of the same name which became such a favourite commodity of smugglers. Tobacco (including Shag and Virginian) was also popular. Ireland was a venue for tobacco and so was Wales.

The cutter, *Eliza*, of Jersey, spent much of 1848 smuggling tobacco and brandy from Jersey to Wales. Of course some boats were caught. On a wild day in 1849 the preventatives (as customs officials were called) learned that contraband goods were to be unloaded at Plémont that evening. The sea was too rough for their own boat so they borrowed a steam paddle tug named *Polka* and made their way around to Plémont. There they found the Jersey cutter, *Lion*, loaded full of brandy. The smugglers, caught red-handed, could think of no satisfactory explanation for their full cargoe of spirits. Some years later on a dark windy night in 1870 the cutter *Mary* from Jersey was caught in Rocquaine Bay off Guernsey smuggling bales of both leaf and manufactured Kentucky tobacco.

Items smuggled by Jersey folk ranged from the strange through the unusual to the bizarre and stories range from the ridiculous through the unbelievable to the tragic. One of the saddest and most extraordinary tales was that of the fishing smack *The Pitt*, named, ironically, after William Pitt the Younger, the English Prime Minister who, in 1783, had decreased duties and increased customs efficiency in order to combat smuggling. *The Pitt* set sail from Jersey in November 1819 bound for Falmouth. She was carrying a cargo of cattle and fifteen passengers. The ship never reached Cornwall. In bad weather *The Pitt* was wrecked on the north-west coast of Guernsey. Twelve of the passengers, eleven women and one man, mostly Irish, were drowned. When they were recovered the female bodies were found to have £1,000 worth of silks wrapped around them under their ordinary clothes. Women were never searched, and therefore, with their more voluminous items of apparel, made ideal smugglers for silks which were a prized commodity. Tragically, in this case, the weight and the con-fining element of the silks had dragged the women down to a watery grave.

One of the most bizarre contraband items has to have been bicycle tyres. These were smuggled from Jersey to France after the end of the Second World War in exchange for French brandy, perfume and nylon stockings; much to the amusement of the magazine *The Yachtsman*. The brandy, however, must have been preferable to the *Trois Six* which was exchanged for smuggled tobacco during the nineteenth century. *Trois Six* was made from distilled beetroot and was described as '... very potent and deletorious to the health of all but metal lined people ...'

King John is mostly known to the English as a 'bad king' through the legends of Robin Hood; losing the Crown Jewels in The Wash on the Norfolk coast; and being forced by his barons to sign Magna Carta in 1215 which was basically an early charter of civil liberties. In the Channel Islands, however, King John is more kindly thought of for his granting of generous privileges when the Islands decided to continue remaining loyal to the English crown after the King had managed to lose Normandy back to the French. One of those privileges was the right to export to England without being liable for customs dues of any kind which allowed the Islanders to openly sell contraband goods to English smugglers.

There was something of the Boys Own daring cavalier about the smugglers simply trying to provide a decent drink and a good smoke for their fellow men, or avoiding ridiculously high taxes on tea and textiles, and many simply turned a good natured blind eye. There was, and is, after all, something infinitely satisfying about 'putting one over' on the Chancellor of the Exchequer; but today, smuggling has taken a sinister downturn. There are fortunes to be made from smuggling drugs and trading in other people's misery and there is no romance, glamour or daring about that.

CHAPTER 12

The Disloyal Dean
1624

... he crashed on to the rocks, and broke all his bones ...

It almost seemed as if Dean David Bandinel was deter-mined to get his name into the history books one way or another. Of Italian birth, he arrived in Jersey in 1601 and by September of that year he was a minister in St Brelade, '... commissioned to preach bareheaded ...' In November 1601 he was appointed Rector of St Brelade and in August 1602 he became a naturalised British subject. He became unpopular in 1607–8 after insisting that a tithe be paid on all fish caught by local fishermen instead of just on the fish they caught in the parish bays. His full title was now Dr The Rev David Bandinel. He sub-sequently became Rector of St Martin's and then he became the first Dean of Jersey in 1620 when James I restored the deanship which had been abolished after the adoption of the Genevan way of worship. One of the perks of this position was that he received the 'great tithes of St Saviours'.

Sir Philippe de Carteret had been born on Sercq (Sark) in 1584, a descendant of one of the twenty sons of Margaret de Carteret (nee Harliston) who had ridden to England to beg Henry VII for her husband's life (see Chapter 4). When he reached manhood he became, first, a Jurat of Jersey and then, in 1626, its Bailiff. Sir Philippe, however, was a haughty and aloof man and along the way he made enemies. One of them was Dean Bandinel who was a violent opponent of Sir Philippe. Sir Philippe retaliated by depriv-ing the Dean of some of his titles and this served to increase the hostility between the two men.

David Bandinel's son, Jacques, was the Rector of St Mary's, one of the smaller parishes on Jersey. More renowned for its sheep breeding than anything else, St Mary's somehow managed to have its rural peace broken often by the somewhat unlikely cause of fierce quarrels between the local constables and the local rectors. St Mary's fifteen minutes of fame came in 1626, the year that de Carteret had become Bailiff, when there was an unusually unpleasant quarrel between the Dean, and the parish Constable. According to the allegations the Constable had gone to St Mary's Church and, according to the Dean, had entered the church '... presuming without any warrant or warning to command him not to preach that day, expelling the clerks, and causing the church to be shut up the whole day to the great scandal of the isle ...' Furthermore, he had forced the Dean's wife out of the church '... at the point of a halberd ...' and had then '... gone on to profane the church and the Communion table with the blood of a dog which he stabbed with a knife while the Minister was preaching ...'

It seems the Constable was making a statement, the point of which was clearly rooted in Philippe de Carteret's dislike of the Dean and also in the fact that though Jersey had been Protestant since Edward Seymour's governorship nearly 100 years before, it tended towards the teachings of Calvin and Luther, and both the Bailiff and the Constable felt that Dean Bandinel was forcing Anglicanism on them. Religion was still a vital issue for it was only twenty-five years since the death of that most Protestant of queens, Elizabeth I, in whose reign the edict was laid down in the Constitution that England should never have another Catholic sovereign. The Catholicism of the kings who followed her, James I and Charles I, was an open secret.

Whatever Dean Bandinel's real religious beliefs were it did not stop him siding with Oliver Cromwell's Parliamentarians during the Civil War (1640–1649) who were Low Church to the point of Puritanism. The Dean helped to block some of the supplies being sent to Mont Orgueil and Elizabeth Castle which Philippe de Carteret and his wife were holding for the King. God moves in mysterious ways for De Carteret became mortally ill but the Dean refused him both the ministrations of a medical man or a minister and the chance to see his wife. By the time Philippe's wife was allowed to see him again he couldn't speak and only managed to raise his hand to her as a sign of recognition. Philippe de Carteret died aged sixty on 23 August 1643.

Meanwhile, Sir Philippe's nephew, Sir George de Carteret, born in 1599 and doubtless another descendant of the indefatigable

The fearsome Mont Orgueil Castle from which Dean Bandinel and his son attempted to escape in 1646. The author

Margaret, who had joined the Navy and attained the rank of captain, had been running an efficient arms supply service between France, Jersey and the West Country in support of the king. When the king heard of Sir Philippe's death, he gave George de Carteret a knighthood and appointed him Lieutenant Governor of Jersey. Sir George had a fearsome reputation and he did much damage to the Parliamentarian cause by sending out a number of privateers masquerading as Parliamentarians.

The Dean's open show of support for Cromwell proved to be his downfall. He and Jacques were imprisoned for their beliefs in Cromwell's ideas of democracy and charged with high treason. They were held in Elizabeth Castle at first and then transferred to Mont Orgueil (Gorey Castle) which had been held by Lady de Carteret for the Royalists at the beginning of the Civil War. Jersey had now firmly declared for the King and there was no room for traitors. The Dean and his son, firmly convinced they would be hung for being Parliamentarians, plotted their escape. On 10 February 1644 they made their attempt.

The chapel crypt at Mont Orgueil Castle where the Dean and his son were imprisoned during the Civil War. From an image of c.1900. Author's collection

The best account of what happened is given by J Chevalier in his *Journal* which he kept between 1643–51 and which was published by the Société Jersiaise in 1915. Chevalier wrote:

> *. . . with a gimlet they bored holes through the plank of a door, and by boring them close together they brake that plank. The door led to another room, next to the outer wall, which had a closet, into which, by removing some stones, they crept with difficulty. Here was a narrow window, through which they had to work hard to squeeze. Then, by the help of a cord and towels fastened to a kitchen ladle fixed in a crack in the wall, they began to climb down. The wall was high and terrifying to descend, and they chose a night when a fierce gale was blowing, and trees were torn up by their roots. At the foot of the wall was rugged rock sore difficult to clamber down. The son [Jacques] slid down first; but the rope was too short, and he fell on the rock and lay senseless. When the father was halfway down, the rope snapped, and he crashed on to the rocks, and broke all his bones . . .*

The Dean was found unconscious the next morning and he died a few hours later. Jacques crawled away from the castle but he too was badly injured. He hid at a friends house deep in the heart of

Jersey but he was recaptured, although he died of his injuries and a fever on 26 July 1644 before he could be put to swing on the end of a rope. It was a tragic end to their daring plan which must have taken a lot of courage to execute. The pair gained little in life from their efforts but earned themselves a place in the folklore and history of Jersey.

In 1649 Charles I was beheaded. Sir George de Carteret then proclaimed Charles's son King Charles II. The monarchy was not officially restored until 1660 but the irony was that the restoration took place under a parliamentary system close to that which Cromwell had envisaged and which still endures today. Charles II visited Jersey and Sir George was rewarded for his loyal services with lands close to present day New York in the 'New World' of North America. He named his dominions New Jersey in honour of his homeland.

CHAPTER 13

Geoffrey's Leap
1646

... the executioner picked up Geoffrey as though he were just a child and threw him over the edge of the cliff, sending him tumbling down into the sea ...

Aperquage was the sanctuary path which ran from a church down to a given point on the coast. Criminals could use this sanctuary path to escape the consequences of the law for no one could touch them while they used it. Several Jersey churches have them and they are believed to be a feature unique to Jersey. The shortest one on the island is a cobbled path which runs a few yards from the Fisherman's Chapel, behind the parish church of St Brelade, its whitewashed walls adorned with frescoes, to the beach below. Here, anyone could escape by taking a boat to France just sixteen miles away. St Clement's, St Ouens, St John's, St Mary's, St Peter's, St Helier's, and St Martin's churches all had perquages.

St Martin was a quiet enough parish most of the time but, as in all small and isolated communities, hidden passions lurked not far beneath the surface and sometimes they spilled over. The parish church dates back to the twelfth century and was dedicated to St Martin of Tours. Grouville Church was dedicated to him as well, giving some idea of his importance in medieval times. One night in 1616, during a violent thunderstorm, the tall spire of St Martin's parish church was struck by lightening and split spectacularly into two parts. To the horrified and superstitious islanders this was a message from God. He was warning them. They believed that the church was struck as a sign that something evil would happen, that some foul deed would be committed and that God wanted to warn them that they must be vigilant. So the St Martin islanders

Le Perquage Ancient Sanctuary Path, behind the fisherman's chapel at St Brelades Church, Jersey. The author

took extra care and they watched and they waited. In 1640 the English Civil War had begun. Jersey was firmly Royalist and declared for the King. Was this what God had warned them about, they wondered, but then they decided that He would have split every church tower on the island with lightening if that was the case. No. It would be an event local to St Martin. That was why He had only split the church tower at St Martin. They would just have to watch and wait.

They had to wait, as it turned out, for three decades after the lightning strike in 1616. Thirty years later, in 1646, Thomas Le Seeleur, a local man, was convicted of burglary and, in times rather harsher than ours at meting out punishments, was sentenced to death. Thomas took the modern view that burglary was not a capital crime, and he escaped being hanged by simply walking the 'sanctuary path of legend', the perquage, which led from the church along a tree-lined lane and down St Catherine's Valley to the coast; and a waiting boat which took him to Normandy and freedom. The islanders watched him go. Was this all that God had been worried about when He sent them the sign by striking their church tower with lightning?

However, Thomas Le Seeleur was not the only person to wish to escape the long arm of the law in 1646. Another criminal, known only as Geoffrey, had committed a '. . . deed most heinous . . .' He had violently attacked and raped a woman. This then was regarded as a capital crime which merited capital punishment. Geoffrey was sentenced to death, but not by hanging which was for 'lesser crimes'. He was to be thrown into the sea from high rocky cliffs at a point between Gorey and Anne Port.

Friends of Geoffrey told him that a way could be found to smuggle him to the sanctuary path from where he could walk to freedom like Thomas Le Seelur. The sanctuary path was as sacred as sanctuary sought in a church. No one, they told him, not even the King himself, would dare to arrest a person on the sanctuary path. Geoffrey was a rather brash and cocksure young man. He couldn't really see what all the fuss was about. His victim was only a woman and all he'd wanted was a bit of fun. If she hadn't resisted so much there wouldn't have been much of a problem. However, he declined to use the perquage path, preferring to brave out his punishment because he was sure that he could escape death.

The day appointed for Geoffrey's execution arrived. Many of the islanders had arrived to watch the proceedings. The folk of St Martin now felt confident that this was the event that had merited the lightening strike. God, all knowing, had seen thirty years into the future and had tried to warn His flock of unsavoury events which would come to pass in their parish perhaps in the vain hope that tragedy could somehow be avoided. Geoffrey was escorted up the cliffs by two strong halberdiers (armed guards) and handed over to the executioner, a big heavy man who wore a heavy brown leather mask to disguise his identity.

The executioner dragged Geoffrey to the top of a rocky outcrop and stood him poised on the edge. The crowd roared approval and with that the executioner picked up Geoffrey as though he were just a child and threw him over the edge of the cliff, sending him tumbling down into the sea. To everyone's amazement, however, Geoffrey was not killed. Despite the height, he seemed to have executed a perfect dive and as he surfaced he started swimming for the shore.

Pandemonium broke out. Some of the ladies present (who probably included outraged friends of the victim) yelled that the executioner was totally inept and that Geoffrey should be thrown off the cliffs again, properly this time. Other folk shouted back that the sentence had been duly carried out, justice had been seen to be

Geoffrey's Leap, near Anne Port where Geoffrey was 'thrown to his death' but survived. The author

done, and Geoffrey should now go free. He could not be tried or punished twice for the same crime.

If Geoffrey had been content to leave it at that he would probably have been allowed to walk unmolested into his future and the obscurity of history. Geoffrey, however, could not resist the chance to show off. He would settle all the arguments, he said, by throwing himself off the cliffs again and showing them how easily the dive could be done. This time Geoffrey walked up to the cliff top unaided, stood poised for a moment on the edge, took a deep breath and launched himself into space. Unfortunately, in his bravado, he slightly misjudged the launch angle and his head struck a rock on the way down. Geoffrey was dead before he hit the water.

All the old clichés come to mind – 'poetic justice', 'what goes around comes around', 'divine retribution'. However, if Geoffrey had died on the first attempt, or had simply walked away a free man after emerging unscathed from the sea, there would have been no story. As it is he earned himself a small place in folklore history.

[See Chapter 18 on William Hales who cheated the hangman and was set free.]

Chapter 14

A Military Madness
1690

*... people are so terrified ... as they
dare not complain for fear of being
murthered.*

Jersey, being nearer to France, had always been more
vulnerable to attack than the Guernsey bailiwick, and
when William of Orange (William III of England) came
to the throne in 1688 he was very aware of this and he decided that
Jersey must be properly defended. Also at the back of his mind
must have been the possible threat posed by the exiled Catholic
monarch, James II, to whom France had given sanctuary. Even
though William was married to James' very Protestant elder
daughter, Mary II of England, he knew that he was vulnerable to
attack by the French. To protect Jersey properly was a laudable aim
but, as with so much else, what seems to be a good idea at the time
can go horribly wrong. William was not a disorganised monarch; he
was, in fact, very much a military man. However, it is unlikely that
he was responsible for planning the defence of Jersey. He would
have delegated it to a trusted member of military staff and it seems
to have been at this point that the seeds of disaster were sown.

Before the days of national newspapers that were widely avail-
able people got their various points across by means of publishing
and distributing pamphlets. On Jersey in 1690 such a pamphlet
was published bearing the punchy title 'The Complaint of the
Inhabitants of the Island of Jersey of the Oppressions and Vio-
lences Committed by the Officers and Soldiers of the Garrison
there.' It offers a rare eye witness account from 300 years ago of
what it was like to be occupied by a military garrison. The dif-
ference from occupation by the Germans in 1940 was that this
occupation was by their own side and in peace time for their own
protection; or so it was supposed.

The first thing that the new military commanders from England did upon arriving in Jersey was to evict the Jersiaise garrison from their comfortable quarters in the castles and fortifications around the island and, without so much as a by-your-leave to the Island government, stamped their own mark of authority on the military matters of Jersey. They then quartered soldiers with the inhabitants so that even those who had homes on the island were living at someone else's expense. Many island soldiers had wives and some of the incomers had brought their wives with them and they were quartered with their husbands, also at the expense of islanders.

Between January 1688 and January 1689 four of the island's seven Companies had been quartered with islanders; the remainder were quartered on the island between January 1689 and June 1690. At the beginning of 1690 all soldiers were given subsistence rates so that they could be 'lodged and dieted', but most refused to pay their unwilling hosts, preferring to drink and gamble the money away instead. When their hosts remonstrated with them many soldiers '... behaved themselves insolently and cruelly ...' Things came to a head when an eighth company of soldiers arrived in Jersey on 8 April 1690 and were also quartered with the hard-pressed inhabitants.

By the end of the first week in June the officers began to seriously fear mass civil disobedience and ordered all junior personnel to camp within the grounds of the island castles. This was not at all to the liking of the disorderly soldiers. Within a month they had destroyed all the bedding and barracks allocated by the officers quartered in the castles and so had to be billetted upon the islanders once more. The officers also withheld the money allocated for the subsistence expenses of the eighth company to arrive, saying that they were not the same regiment and making other silly bureaucratic excuses. Supply ships arrived in Jersey, carrying provisions and building materials, which were diverted by the military commanders for their own uses.

The situation began to deteriorate rapidly as the islanders began to starve. The pamphlet describes it rather more vividly:

> ... *divers crimes of the highest nature have been committed by the officers and soldiers of the garrison upon the persons of the inhabitants ... both officers and soldiers have come to such an excess of boldness as to villifie openly the Civil magistrates, abuse the Ministers of the Gospel, beat the Constables, and in open market to run with their*

swords drawn upon sundry of the inhabitants ... beat 'em and affront 'em ... and also the soldiers going into the shambles, taking by force and violence the meat from the butchers and ... likewise the fish from the fishermen ... without paying ... and ... great many houses having been broken, and goods stolen ... people are so terrified ... as they dare not complain for fear of being murthered.

Things could not go on like this. The islanders were living in fear and dread and many were on the point of starvation. Ordinary people were in awe and often scared of the soldiers, knowing how easy it would be for the military to throw them into the castle dungeons on some pretext or other. Livelihoods were being ruined, drunkenness was rife, there was much molesting and the occasional rape of island women and literal daylight robbery was common. The soldiers ran amok in St Helier most days and every night. Their commanders either couldn't or wouldn't curb their excesses. Something had to break the vicious cycle which seemed to have wrapped itself around daily living. What finally broke it was the bravery of the local Deputies. Appalled at what was happening they volubly demanded justice for the islanders and, deaf to all threats, eventually promised that they would sail to England and complain personally to the King about the havoc that his military forces were wreaking on Jersey. After all, they were his loyal subjects and the King was not at war with them and yet they were suffering more cruelly than if he had been fighting them.

Soldiers running amok in St Helier during a military madness, 1780. Courtesy of the artist, H Niblett

It was a slow process but common sense finally prevailed and the worst offenders were brought to justice. The islanders found it hard to forgive or forget but gradually life began to return to normal. It was a tragedy that it all ever got that far. Though undoubtedly brave, the Deputies seem to have been very slow in reacting to the plight of the ordinary people. The commanding officers were not going to argue too much. They knew William for a harsh man when he was riled, as the Irish could testify, and it is unbelievable that they could allow Jersey, who was not the enemy, to be treated so badly by its protecting forces in a time of peace.

Chapter 15

A Jersey Tragedy
1695

*Rushing into Marie's room he shouted
forth a torrent of hatred at her and,
raising his sword, he blindly struck
three savage blows to her chest ...*

Samuel de la Place was Rector of St Mary's on Jersey and a
strict churchman. This had led him to refuse to recognise
David Bandinel's elevation to the position of Dean of
Jersey in 1620, a deanery endowed by the 'Great Tithes of St
Saviours', as the old Calvinist doctrine was gradually replaced by
the Anglican one during the early 1620s. Besides there was no
position of Dean mentioned in the Scriptures, argued Samuel,
somewhat unsuccessfully, for he found himself replaced as Rector
of St Marys in 1620, by, much to his chagrin, Jacques Bandinel,
another member of the large Bandinel family whose members
seemed to have a predilection for professions within the Church.

The Bandinels were an Italian family, liked by some on the
Island, resented by others. Jacques Bandinel married a Jersey girl
named Judith Bonhomme, who was the daughter of Josué Bonhomme, the Rector of St Lawrence. Together they had seven
children and then moved to Guernsey. Their son, Josué, however,
returned to Jersey to become Rector of Trinity in 1642. He succeeded yet another Bandinel churchman, Jean Bandinel, who had
only been appointed to that post the year before. It was, however,
the time of the English Civil War and Jean Bandinel had found
himself supporting the wrong side.

Josué settled in Trinity. In due course he too married and had
three children: Pierre, Susanne and Marie. Pierre grew up to
become the Rector of St Lawrence's Church whose sixth-century
patron saint had died so horribly. Even today his suffering is still
commemorated by the emblem of the rack depicted on the parish

St Mary's Church, where Samuel de la Place was rector before being replaced by Jaques Bandinel. The author

flag of St Lawrence. In the early 1690s Marie married a Guernsey-man, Josué Guille, and they settled down to married life together on Jersey.

Josué and Marie were desperate to start a family, and sometimes it caused tensions between them. When Marie finally did become pregnant they were absolutely overjoyed. Josué looked forward to having his son very much and he planned what they would do together when the boy was old enough. His son would carry his name and when he grew up he would inherit Josué's estates and raise his own family there in turn and so the family line would be perpetuated. Josué could not bear the thought that his name might just die out. Marie looked forward to simply starting her family. Secretly she didn't really mind whether the child was a boy or a girl just so long as it was strong and healthy. This after all was the seventeenth century. Antibiotics were unknown and many children died in infancy. It was a case of survival of the fittest.

At last all Josué and Maria's time of waiting was rewarded by the birth of a baby boy. Josué was delighted. Now at last he had his son. Marie, although weak after the birth, adored her baby and gazed long and lovingly at him as he suckled her breast. Unfortunately, however, fate was not on their side. The baby was not strong. He was sickly and he did not thrive. Early one morning soon after his birth he died, leaving Josué and Marie heartbroken. Marie sobbed quietly to herself while Josué raged at the unfairness of losing his longed for son. Someone had to be responsible for his loss. Someone had to be to blame. Suddenly he saw it all with dreadful clarity. The baby had depended upon his mother. She was the one who cared for him and looked after him so if some mishap had befallen him she was the one who was at fault. Only it wasn't just some mishap. His son was dead. Therefore his mother must have let him down in some terrible way. She had ultimately betrayed both of them. Shaking with grief and anger Josué seized his sword. He could not bring his son back but, by God! he would avenge him. Rushing into Marie's room he shouted forth a torrent of hatred at her and, raising his sword, he blindly struck three savage blows to her chest. Marie screamed as she was felled by the blows. Collapsing in a heap on the floor, she died almost at once from the loss of blood caused by her injuries.

The commotion brought family and neighbours running to the scene where they stared in horror and disbelief at Josué holding his bloody sword and the crumpled butchered body of Marie which lay on the floor in front of them. Retribution was swift. Josué was arrested at once. The inquest was held and Royal Court proceedings were initiated on the same day that Marie had died. Twelve jurors were appointed and the trial began on 11 September 1695. Josué confessed that he had killed Marie because of his acute distress over the death of his child. He was quickly found guilty and justice was dispensed the same day as the trial. Josué was sentenced to death. He was taken to Gallows Hill for execution and there he was publicly strangled. He had killed his wife and he had no son and so his estates were confiscated by the Crown and his name was lost. That which he had most feared he had brought about by his own hand.

Chapter 16

Jersey's 'Legal Pirates'
1700s

*... in 1778 twenty Jersey privateers
took shipping and goods worth
£343,500 sterling ...*

Privateering was a legalised form of pirating and it made many Channel Island folk very rich between 1689 (when it began) and 1856 (when it was finally abolished); especially during the eighteenth century. A privateer was a ship adapted for warfare by a private individual or a group of individuals who were not part of the official fighting forces. Such ships were sanctioned by the Crown to attack and raid enemy shipping. Any type of ship could be used from smacks to frigates; but the main types used were cutters and schooners because of their speed. Cutters were also frequently used by customs officers because of their ability to outrun most other ships.

The first real privateer on Jersey, however, was not an islander, but a Spaniard. Almost 400 years earlier, in 1406, Pero Niño, a Spanish 'soldier of fortune' sailed into port and, with the help of a Frenchman, Hector de Pontbriant, defeated the Jersey militia. In later centuries most privateers simply took ships for ransom and treasure, but Pero Niño took the whole island. After he took control of Jersey he extorted a ransom of 10,000 golden arrows and an annual tribute of twelve lances, twelve axes, twelve bows and twelve trumpets. Then he sailed away, a rich man by the standards of his day.

By the seventeenth century Jersey had suffered badly from a number of such raids, mainly by the French. There was bitter resentment among the islanders and petitions were sent to the King. Ironically, it was a Dutch King of England, William III of Orange, married to the English Queen Mary II, who signed the first privateering authorisations. The Dutch had suffered badly from raids on their shipping during the English Civil War less than half a century before. However, since the King received 20 per cent of the value of ships and treasure seized, he had a vested interest.

Authorisation was in the form of a *Letter of Marque* signed by the King. There were proper *Articles of Agreement* between the owner(s) of the ship and the officers and crew. Fourteen clauses laid down terms and conditions and how many shares in goods and cargoes seized should be received by each crew member. This could be dependent on rank and also on the contribution made by each crew member to a particular 'cruise' as their armed expeditions were known. After the king had taken his share, two thirds of the remainder went to the owners which left four fifteenths to be divided between the crew.

Although Jersey was not as effective at privateering as its sister island of Guernsey, nevertheless, Jersey privateers had taken 151 ships by 1711, and during the Seven Years War over £60,000 sterling was taken (worth around £4 million pounds at today's value). The privateers were only allowed to attack ships of His Majesty's enemies, which, at this point in time, were France and Spain. In the 1760s, while the American War of Independence was raging, Jerseymen held 150 French ships in St Aubin's Bay; and then, taking a leaf out of Pero Niño's book, went on land forays as well. One raid on Caën netted them oxen, cows, sheep, and, with a rare touch of humour, all the washing of a local clergyman and his two washerwomen. The privateers took an American ship, *The Snipe*, in 1812 which was a good example for illustrating the range and richness of goods carried that could be seized and auctioned. *The Snipe*'s cargo included sugar, spices, cotton, cocoa, coffee, pepper, indigo and 146 bear skins.

One of the most successful privateering ships was *The Charming Nancy* which began life as a French vessel, named *Le St Clement*, until she was captured in 1745 by a Jersey privateer, Michael Le Pape. During three months (October to December, 1747) she captured and brought home five ships into St Aubin. These were: a Portuguese ship, *La Notre Dame du Rozaire*; *The Elizabeth* from Scarborough; *La Dame Gertrude D'Amsterdam*; *Le Heron* of St Malo; and *The John and Mary* from Normandy. Cargoes included salt, cotton, brandy, wine, tobacco, wood, skins, tar and pitch.

Clause Seven of the Articles of Agreement between a privateering ship's owners and its crew, stated that there should be no plundering, which seems absurd, given that this was the whole aim of the attacks made by these privateers; but it doubtless referred to the case that once the captured cargo was on board, individual crew members should not help themselves but were to wait until the official shareout; thereby confirming the old saying about 'honour among thieves'. This indictment may seem rather harsh, but there is good reason. The intention of licensing privateers was to give French, Spanish and (during the War of Independence) American shipping a hard time and to recoup some of the losses incurred during the fighting that occurred between these nations and England during the eighteenth century, as well as acting as spies and gathering information which might be useful to the English government. Of course it didn't work that way. Some privateers became over zealous or simply plain greedy and began attacking ships of both friendly and neutral nations indiscriminately.

First to complain were the Dutch whose King William of Orange, had sat on the English throne as King William III and ruled the country jointly with his wife, Mary II, Queen of England. The Dutch had been confident that this uniting of the two countries would bring an end to the offensive on their shipping by the English. William had, in fact, signed some of the earliest official privateering orders. However he and Mary had no children. She died in 1695 and when William died in 1702 the throne passed to Mary's younger sister, Anne. A few decades later Dutch ships were being plundered once more by the privateers from the Channel Islands who were supposed to owe their allegiance to the English crown.

The Dutch grievances were followed by complaints from Denmark, Tuscany, Egypt, Turkey and the Ottoman Empire. Finally, the privateers began attacking English ships. In 1777, a kind of 'bail system' was introduced whereby owners of privateers had to pay a deposit of £1,500 (for a ship with a crew of less than 150) or £3,000 (for ships which had larger crews) which would be forfeited if their ship attacked the shipping of any country which was not at war with England and which was not an enemy. This measure clearly did not work, however, for the attacks continued and the commanders of privateers encouraged the defection of English sailors to privateering by bribing them with the offer of large bounties. The following year, in November 1778, a warning was issued by George III that misuse of a *Letter of Marque* in this way would incur '. . . our [the king's] highest displeasure and such penalty as by law may be inflicted . . .'

A month later, a clearly exasperated George III, who had already given privateers a warning about attacking ships of the Ottoman Empire and subjects of the 'Grand Signor', issued a much more serious warning:

> . . . whereas Commanders of merchant ships that have obtained Letters of Marque are authorised to take only ships, etc., belonging to the French King or his vassals and subjects and in no wise to attempt anything against the ships, etc., or any other prince or state in amity with us. Notwithstanding which we have received divers complaints of great irregularities and unjustifiable violences committed by our privateers by seizing the ships etc., of the subjects of such princes and states. For the avoiding for the future all such irregularities and to remove every possible cause for complaint we do hereby strictly charge and enjoin the commanders and crews of all vessels having Letters of Marque that they do not under any pretence seize or detain any such ship etc. (such goods not being warlike or naval stores) unless they shall have probable ground to suspect that the evidence offered as to the property of such ship and goods is fraudulent and untrue . . . and it having been particularly represented unto us, that notwithstanding the orders which we have given to prevent the capture of any Dutch ships laden with innocent cargoes, vessels of that description continue to be taken . . . we do hereby strictly charge the commanders of such privateers that they do not on any account seize or detain any ship belonging either to the States-General [Holland] of the United Provinces or their subjects . . .

George III's dilemma however was that the privateers were out of control and Letters of Marque were a recipe open to widely differing interpretations. The king had his own problems as well in that he had developed a serious medical condition which appeared to rob him of his sanity and for much of the latter part of his reign his eldest son, who was to become George IV, acted as Regent. Modern doctors believe that George III suffered from an aversion to sunlight. The doctors of the time, however, not realising this, recommended that the king take as much fresh air and sunshine as possible which simply made his condition worse.

Meanwhile, this left the privateers to do pretty much as they pleased. In 1778, twenty Jersey privateers took shipping and goods worth £343,500 sterling (worth around £17,175,000 sterling at today's values). The following year six privateers took £270,000 sterling (worth £13,500,000 sterling at today's values); and three years after that in 1782 just five privateers scooped pickings of £156,000 sterling (worth around £10,550,000 sterling at today's values). The French suffered particularly badly and the Governor of Cherbourg remarked rather desperately that '... these islands [Channel Islands] are the despair of France ... through their remarkably active privateers ...'

The amount of money brought into the Bailiwick through privateering activities was phenomenal. Many fine houses were built on the island during the privateering era, characterised by the architectural style of five windows across the top storey and two windows on either side of the front door, making a total of nine windows. It was big business and the finance industry eighteenth century style. In retrospect the Bailiwick was lucky that the legitimately aggrieved nations (i.e. the non enemies of the English Crown) such as the Dutch, the Danish and the Ottoman Empire, did not declare war on Jersey as the Dutch had threatened to do in the Isles of Silly during the Civil War. If that had happened the Channel Islands might have forfeited the medieval privileges granted by King John which they enjoy to this day.

There was, however, a price to pay. The French fought back, bravely and bitterly, and the cost to Jersey was the loss of two thirds of her shipping. For Jersey the defeat of Napoleon in 1815 effectively signalled the end of the island's privateering era. Privateering was eventually officially abolished in 1856 by international agreement, but many innocent foreign merchants and businessmen from countries friendly to England, and even from England herself, had been ruined by the avaricious greed, and sometimes by the lack of conscience, on the part of those privateers who would sell the ship's crew or pressgang them into service on ships belonging to the mother country of the privateers; neither of which they were legally permitted to do. Much of the time privateering was little better than a semi-legalised form of pirating which had long been an unofficial profession in the Channel Islands.

CHAPTER 17

A Jilted Bride
c.1800

The bells had ceased their joyous pealing and an unusual quietness lay over the Valley.

St Lawrence, Jersey's 'central parish', which lies to the west of St Helier and borders St Aubin's Bay, should be nothing more than a pretty and peaceful rural parish, with the picturesque thirteenth century church lying at its heart. It is home to Tiger Park which boasts hedges clipped into tiger shapes and the original cars used in the *Bergerac* detective series and the film *Goldfinger*. Incongruously hidden away in the countryside close by, is the Rwanda Consulate guarded by high automatic gates and a pair of cannon. St Lawrence, however, has also managed to attract more than a touch of the macabre to itself. First there was the 'Hangman's Cottage', the home of the island's public executioner, which lay between Mainland and Bel Royal. Then were the sinister tunnels of the German Underground Hospital with their entombed dead, but that is another story. There was however another place and another story which, in the minds of many islanders, eclipsed even these horrors. To them the saddest and perhaps even foulest deed was the tragedy of a young girl who is said to haunt the Waterworks Valley.

Stories like hers, and that of Jeanne in *The Cry of the Tombelènes* are passed down through oral tradition and, like Chinese Whispers, details get altered or rearranged or forgotten in the re-telling. One such detail in this story was the girl's real name but her Christian name is thought to have been Marie. Marie was a traditionally pretty Jersey girl with dark hair and brown eyes. Little is known of her fiancé. He may have been local or he might have been one of the many soldiers garrisoning the island. This story happened just over 200 years ago when Napoleon was terrorising

France and much of the rest of Europe; and Jersey was heavily fortified against possible attack.

The Waterworks Valley is an ugly name for a most beautiful place. The valley runs through the heart of St Lawrence and takes its name from the nineteenth century reservoirs of Millbrook (4.5 km long) and Handois; and the Dannemarsh Reservoir, built in 1901. They are fed by a wide stream whose waters used to work six water mills from which Le Chemin des Moulins road takes its name. Close to the Dannemarsh Reservoir stands the Hamptonne Country Life Museum which includes 300 years of Jersey's rural history and reconstructions of seventeenth and eighteenth century Jersey farmhouses, much like the one in which Marie would have lived. The valley itself is like stepping back into history. There are woodlands, flowers, blackberry bushes, meadows intersected with turf covered lanes, all overgrown, pretty and picturesque, much like the old greenwoods must have been in King John and Robin Hood's time.

Marie was one of those people who love once and only once in their lives. When she gave her heart it was quite literally forever. She was very excited about her forthcoming wedding and she planned everything to the last detail. Her friends helped her with

Waterworks Valley, St Lawrence, c.1920. Author's collection

WATERWORKS VALLEY,
JERSEY.   21

Marie going to her wedding, being driven down the Waterworks Valley in her coach.
Courtesy of the artist, H Niblett

her wedding trousseau. There were no such things as wedding present lists and department stores in the eighteenth century. Each bride was expected to hem her own sheets, embroider her own pillowcases, quilt her own bedcovers, make her own frocks, night-dresses, underwear and knit her own stockings for her married life.

Marie's parents were dead and so on her wedding morning she dressed carefully by herself in front of the long mirror which her mother had so prized when she was alive. She wore a pretty sprigged muslin dress with short puffed sleeves and a fine shawl lay across her shoulders. She had wound flowers into her hair and around her neck lay the gold locket which her father had given her for her eighteenth birthday. Marie wiped a tear from the corner of her eye. She would so have liked her mother and father with her on this special day. Her parents had left her enough to live comfortably. Outside the house she could see the coach that would take her to her wedding. It had been decorated with bright ribbons and the coachman had tied white ribbons to his whip. It was a beautiful day, full of promise, and she was so in love. The happiest day of her life she thought and she would not be lonely again with a husband at her side to care for her and guide her.

The bells were ringing loud and clear, pealing out across the valley, calling her to the church to be united forever with her beloved fiancé. She got into the coach and they set off down the Waterworks Valley. It was a beautiful drive through the green-

Waterworks Valley, St Lawrence, c.1922. Author's collection

woods, alive with spring flowers and birdsong, and Marie was full of anticipation as they drew up at the church. The lychgate was festooned with colourful garlands of flowers and the granite church looked pretty and tranquil in the sunshine. The clear blue sky overhead promised a perfect day and Marie's face was wreathed in smiles when she got out of the coach. As she arranged her dress the rector came to say that her bridegroom had not yet arrived and would she like to wait outside in the sunshine. Marie shook her head. She wanted to sit in the sweet smelling church scented with the huge bunches of flowers which the villagers had picked that morning. She wanted a few minutes of quiet contemplation before she said her vows. The rector took her arm and led her through the lychgate decorated with its mass of blooms to celebrate her forthcoming marriage and together they entered the church.

An hour passed and Marie was conscious of a faint whispering behind her. She did not look round. She was sure that he would come and she sat, straight-backed, her hands clasped, looking at the altar where she would kneel beside him and become his wife. She did not see the pitying looks that were passing between the assembled wedding guests. After nearly two hours, the rector took her arm and led her into the vestry. Her bridegroom was not

The lychgate at St Lawrence Church decorated with flowers for a twenty-first-century wedding, just like it would have been decorated for Marie's wedding. The author

coming, he told her gently. A message had arrived to say that he was sorry but he could not go through with it and he had left the island. Marie stared at him in complete shock. Her face went white and, unbidden, tears slid slowly down her cheeks. The rector tried his best to comfort her, feeling awkward and not knowing what to say to this young woman who had been so gloriously happy only an hour before. Marie shook her head and tried to smile her thanks through her tears. She did not want his pity. She dried her eyes carefully and, mustering all her dignity and courage, turned and walked slowly back through the church with her head held high, looking to neither right nor left. Marie blinked as she emerged into the bright promising sunshine and walked unseeing back to her coach. The coachman, his eyes carefully averted, helped her in, and she asked him in a steady voice to drive her home again.

The bells had ceased their joyous pealing and an unusual quietness lay over the valley. Alone in her coach, silent tears began to run down Marie's cheeks. Like the legendary fictional heroine, Miss Havisham, of a century later, a heartbroken Marie could not believe the pain of her betrayal. What had she done to deserve this? How could she bear it? Why had he gone? What would she do now? Unlike Miss Havisham, however, Marie could not even begin to think of facing a lifetime alone without the only man she would ever love. On arrival back at the house she went straight to her bedroom and locked the door. There she remained, deaf to all entreaties, refusing to open the door.

Marie would not speak to anyone. She left food and drink untouched outside her bedroom door. No sound came from her

St Lawrence's Church today. The author

room. The servants grieved with her, worried for her, became seriously concerned about her refusal to answer their pleas to let them into the room. Finally they agreed among themselves that something had to be done. A locksmith was fetched and at last he broke the door open. Marie lay motionless on the bed. She was dead. In her terrible heartbreak, and still wearing her wedding dress, she had killed herself. This tragic story has never been forgotten and to this day it is said that a phantom coach carrying a ghostly bride still drives down the Waterworks Valley on the anniversary of what should have been Marie's wedding day.

Chapter 18

You Can't Be Hanged Twice
1807

Hales hanged suspended for a whole minute by his neck but he did not die ...

During the early 1800s, thousands of English soldiers were stationed on Jersey to protect the island from possible attack by Napoleon. Such an attack never came and many of the soldiers found themselves with little to do except to find some way of passing the time on Jersey until they could return to England. For most this meant frequenting the local ale houses and for some the local whore houses. Both these pursuits required money and a few of those who didn't have sufficient funds turned to crime to get them.

One such soldier was William Hales. Bored and fed up, he committed several burglaries to obtain the cash he needed for his pleasures. It was easy to commit the burglaries and then return to the anonymity of his barracks. He would stake out potential victims and watch them for a short while before making his move. It worked well for a while until one day he decided to burgle a local watchmaker's home to fill his purse. Unfortunately for Hales the watchmaker returned home unexpectedly and discovered Hales filling his pockets. In the ensuing struggle Hales killed the watchmaker. Panic stricken he fled but he didn't get very far. He was apprehended by the Island authorities and charged with robbery and murder. Hales denied the whole thing of course but there was sufficient evidence against him for him to be sent to trial. As was to be expected back then he was sentenced to death and the date for his execution set for Saturday 25 April 1807. It was at this point that events occurred which resulted in William Hales entering the history books.

What took place is best described in the words of the *Gazette de L'Île de Jersey* in a report published on Saturday 2 May 1807.

French was then the official language of Jersey so what follows is a translation:

> ... *Last Saturday was the date fixed for the execution of William Hales. He maintained his innocence of the crimes of which he was accused and requested a pardon from God ...*

There follows a brief description of the crowd which had gathered to watch (executions still took place in public at this time), of the hood being placed over Hales's head and the noose put around his neck before the trap door opened and he swung into eternity. At least that is what should have happened but Hales did not appear to be dying very quickly. The *Gazette* takes up the story:

> ... *after the trap door opened Hales hung suspended for a whole minute by his neck but he did not die and to end his suffering the executioner pulled on his feet but the rope slipped and Hales fell to the ground. Nevertheless the executioner tried to reattach the rope but the offender realised what was happening and managed to slip the rope from his neck. This cruel situation excited the crowd's sympathy, for such a thing had never happened before, and they took Hales back to the prison. The following Monday noon the Royal Court decided to give Hales the King's pardon after receiving a petition from the inhabitants* [of Jersey] *for this humanitarian act ...*

Under the Jersey version of the English 'double jeopardy' (no man can be tried twice) which, not unreasonably, stated that no man can be hanged twice, the court had no choice but to give Hales the King's Pardon and he walked from the Courtroom a free man and into the legal history books.

CHAPTER 19

The Apples of Death
1829

Philippe brooded on his cruel treatment by his father and he felt that his childhood had been stolen from him.

Philippe Jolin did not have a happy childhood. He was born on Jersey in 1808 to a farmer and his wife and should perhaps have had an idyllic upbringing. However, times were hard and there was a great fear that the French would attack at any moment. Napoleon was snarling at the island from his kingdom in France and new fortifications were hurriedly being built while the old ones were strengthened. Philippe's father, also called Philippe, was worried and depressed, and he was not in the best of health, suffering from gout and much pain in both his feet. To ease his suffering and to forget (at least temporarily) his worries, he drank, sometimes to excess.

Young Philippe quickly learned the hard way what happened when he got on the wrong side of his father. Philippe Snr would take his belt or his fists to his son at the slightest provocation. Philippe was not alone in being punished in this way. His father treated all his children in the same way. If any of them committed even the slightest misdemeanour he would take off his belt and thrash them, sometimes until they bled. On occasion his mother would try and intervene when Philippe Snr beat his children but then she too would be badly beaten for her trouble. During a couple of particularly vicious attacks by his father Philippe Jnr was beaten around the head with an iron bar. His mother screamed and protested but in vain. Philippe Snr smacked her so hard across the face that she fell over half stunned and he continued with his punishment of his son. This beating may have caused some sort of brain damage for the child became withdrawn and brooding and sometimes his behaviour was noted as being a little odd.

By the time he reached his teens young Philippe had had enough and in 1823 he decided to run away to sea. He kept his eyes and ears open and laid his plans carefully, finally escaping from Jersey and his cruel father on a brig named *The Pelican*. The ship sailed from Jersey to Europe and then onwards to South America. It was an exciting adventure for young Philippe. He enjoyed being at sea, the travelling and seeing new places, but most of all he enjoyed his new found freedom. He was treated as an equal and he no longer had to endure the merciless beatings but somehow he couldn't let go of his past.

Philippe brooded on his cruel treatment by his father and he felt that his childhood had been stolen from him. Sometimes he would be seen staggering around the decks of *The Pelican* as though he were drunk, muttering that he wished he could just throw himself into the sea and never see his parents again. Despite his new found independence and the new lease of life that his shipboard and travelling experiences had given him, Philippe could not resolve his inner turmoil. Finally in 1829, after six years at sea and grown to manhood, he returned to Jersey as an ex-seaman at the tender age of twenty-one.

This was not a wise move for Philippe had a failing. He loved 'alcohol and arguments' as much as his father. Philippe Jnr seems to have made little effort to find a job and, as he was no longer a child, he and his father took to drinking together in the quayside bars of St Helier where they 'argued contentedly' together for hours. Or so it seemed. However, young Philippe had not forgotten the ill treatment and cruelty of his childhood. Resentment festered and simmered just below the surface and it was only a matter of time before something happened which would cause it to boil over. As always, it happened sooner rather than later.

On Monday 7 September Philippe Jnr wandered into town as usual, and spent the morning drinking, before wandering home again about noon wanting his lunch. No lunch had been prepared for him so, disgruntled, he decided to wander back into town again and continue drinking. By this time the family had had enough of Philippe Jnr's lazy and alcoholic ways and Philippe Snr ordered his son not to go. However, his son was a grown man now. He was no longer afraid of his father and not in the least inclined to take orders from him. There was an almighty row and Philippe threatened his father before he set off to go drinking once more.

By the time he returned home again Philippe Jnr was feeling very hungry. After all he had had no lunch and so he went to pick some apples to eat from his father's orchard. The fruit was not yet fully ripe so Philippe Snr became very upset when he saw his son picking the apples. Apples were a valuable crop used for both the making of cider and black butter as well as being a well liked and versatile fruit. A good price could be fetched for them and he wasn't going to put up with people 'scrumping'. Consequently he stormed down to the orchard and began kicking his son. This time Philippe Jnr fought back, shouting and arguing loudly, before walking off down a lane away from the side of the house. His father followed him, yelling at the top of his voice. The argument had now developed into a full scale row.

Neighbour Marie Le Riche, who was then aged twenty-eight, watched them rowing. Philippe Snr bawled out that it was no use Philippe Jnr just going off because he'd find him wherever he was on the island. Philippe Jnr shouted that that was true but the fight wasn't over yet. With that Philippe Jnr stormed over to a nearby building site, picked up two pieces of brick and threw one at his father. The brick hit Philippe Snr on the head, knocking him out, and he crumpled into a heap. Philippe Jnr looked with contempt at his father lying in the lane and muttered 'come on now pick yourself up' before walking off, nonchalantly eating an apple.

By now the effects of his drinking were beginning to tell on young Philippe. Finding a convenient shop doorway he lay down and passed into a drunken stupor. However, unbeknown to him, while he slept off the effects of his excess alcohol in the shop doorway his father was dying from a fatal brain haemorrhage caused by the blow from the brick. When he finally awoke four hours later he found himself arrested on a charge of murder and patricide.

The date for Philippe Jolin's trial was set for Monday 28 September at the Royal Court, presided over by Bailiff Sir Thomas Le Breton. Attorney General John Dupré acted for the Crown Prosecution and Advocate Hammond acted on behalf of Philippe Jolin. There were also twenty-four jurors from St Saviour, St Lawrence and St Helier. Philippe Jolin Jnr pleaded not guilty to murder but guilty to manslaughter.

There were a number of witnesses who offered their testimony:

- Philip Jeune, who had lived in the Jolin household for seven years, said he had witnessed many angry rows.
- Margaret Huard had tried to intervene after Philippe's mother had called for help because his father was hitting Philippe over the head with an iron bar.
- Philip Manuel said Philippe's father had beaten his son round the head with an iron bar and then kicked him as he lay on the ground.
- John Case (aged forty-five) the local blacksmith, had advised Philippe's father to chastise his son with a stick or a piece of cord, not a hammer.
- Philip Aubin, a friend of Philippe Jnr, said that in 1823 the pair were shipmates on *The Pelican*, and that Philippe had acted oddly on board, saying he wanted to throw himself in the sea and never see his parents again. He would lurch around the decks and Aubin was never quite sure if Jolin was drunk or mad.
- Dr M'Doual (of the Royal Navy) who had tried to save Philippe Snr's life, said that, although it was no excuse for what happened, he would have died soon anyway from his gout.

A testimonial was read to the court which said that on 7 January 1825 Philippe Jnr had helped to rescue the crew of the ship *Fanny* when it had been wrecked on Les Buts Rocks near Elizabeth Castle. He had gone to the assistance of the drowning men and brought at least some of them safely to shore. He was therefore a very brave man and did not deserve to hang.

However, sadly for Jolin, the Crown Prosecution lawyer was a better advocate and he said sternly that being drunk was no excuse for murder and a son 'must' respect his father's authority. This was much in keeping with the times just as it was much in keeping with the times that no one had thought to try and prevent such ill-treatment of the child or his siblings and his mother. It was considered that a man had the right to beat his wife and family if he chose to do so. The jury took just fifty-five minutes to find Jolin guilty. The Jurats covered their faces and the prisoner knelt to receive sentence. He was to be hung by the neck until he was dead.

Philippe Jolin pleaded that the drink and the kicking he had received while picking the apples had unhinged him; and he blamed a poor education, drink and the lack of religious guidance for his predicament. Furthermore, he agreed wholeheartedly that the chastisement of children was absolutely necessary. It was to no avail. Philippe Jolin's sad and wasted life came to an end when he was executed on Saturday 3 October 1829 on Gallows Hill (now Westmont) on Jersey.

CHAPTER 20

After Noon
1845

Once in prison Noon went beserk.
He shouted and swore and trashed
his cell.

I n the nineteenth century, St Helier was a busy trading port. Hundreds of ships from all over the world called in to unload cargo, shelter from the weather, to take on provisions, and sometimes just to allow their crews a break ashore to spend their hard earned cash and have a good time. A good time usually involved wine and women. There was often a good deal of drinking and not a few fights. Like most arguments drunken fights would start about something and nothing and would be over within a few minutes; but a few became more serious and one or two escalated out of control. This story involves a drunken squabble which spilled over into something much more serious, several police officers, the Royal Court of Jersey and Centenier George Le Cronier who was to die a few months later at the hands of 'a lady of the night' (see Chapter 2).

The Comus, a coal ship from Hartlepool, captained by a man with the German sounding name of Gotterel, had docked in St Helier on Friday 12 December 1845. John Noon was the First Mate. He was more than ready for a bit of festive cheer with his friends and drinking acquaintances so a group of them arranged to meet the following evening at the *Le Gros Inn* on Mulcaster Street. Coincidentally, this street was the adjacent street to Mulberry Street where Centenier Le Cronier would meet his death. Whereas Mulberry Street has changed beyond recognition, Mulcaster Street remains little altered from the time of this story.

On that fateful Saturday evening Noon had also invited Thomas Hodge, a mate of his from the schooner *The Syren* (which was also in port), to join him for dinner at the *Le Gros Inn*. Thomas accepted. He knew that they kept a good table there. Both men intended to make a long enjoyable evening of it and accordingly both men had booked rooms at the *Le Gros Inn*. After Noon and Hodge had finished their meal other sailors from *The Syren* joined them at their table. As the evening wore on the drink flowed, the laughter and jokes got more ribald, and some of the language used became downright obscene.

Eventually the landlady took exception to their bad language and asked them to quieten down. Noon refused. Then Thomas Hodge hissed at him to at least tone down his language. John Noon ignored his friend and made such a fuss and bother about anyone trying to curb his enjoyment that the landlord finally ordered them to leave. John Noon was by now very drunk and insisted that he wasn't going anywhere. Hodge, a bit more sober and becoming somewhat embarrassed by the situation, tried to hustle Noon out. At that, Noon lost his temper completely, pulled out his knife and slashed Hodge viciously across the thigh. Thomas Hodge staggered back against the door as he fell and shouted a warning: 'I'm stabbed! Mind him!'

Realising that matters had now got seriously out of hand, the landlord sent for the police. First to arrive was Jean de Parcq, a Constable's Officer. He saw at once that the fighting was out of control and sent for assistance. Another Constable's Officer, named Henry Manuel, and Constable Pierre le Sueur, arrived. They broke up the fight and then sent for Dr Dickson. In all the shouting and confusion John Noon had escaped. Thomas Hodge was not so lucky. When Noon had stabbed Hodge he had severed an artery and by the time Dr Dickson arrived Thomas Hodge had bled to death.

At this point Centenier George Le Cronier arrived. It was now a murder case instead of just a bar room brawl. There were plenty of eyewitnesses and it soon became evident that John Noon was the man responsible for Thomas Hodge's death. Le Cronier and the other officers at once set about tracking Noon down. First of all they went straight to the port, located *The Comus* and Le Cronier boarded her. Finding a man asleep, or, judging by the smell of alcohol, passed out in a drunken stupor, Le Cronier left his officers guarding the man and, finding a lantern, fetched other sailors from *The Comus* who were also lodging at the *Le Gros Inn* so that that he could obtain an identification. It was John Noon.

Le Cronier shook Noon roughly awake and told him that he was under arrest. Denying that he was John Noon, Noon started another scuffle and again escaped. Le Cronier was not to be defeated. He ordered the whole quay to be cordoned off and eventually John Noon was caught and taken to prison. Once in prison Noon went beserk. He shouted and swore and trashed his cell. When he was finally dragged out for questioning he refused to say where he had been that evening. The Constable of St Helier, however, decided that he had sufficient evidence in the form of eyewitness accounts to charge John Noon with murder.

On 15 December 1845 John Noon appeared at the Royal Court in front of the Bailiff, Jean de Veulle. Noon's advocate, Monsieur Godfray, entered a plea of 'not guilty' on Noon's behalf. Police Constable Pierre Le Sueur gave his report. Noon's hat was produced which had been found at the *Le Gros Inn* on the night Thomas Hodge died and which had been identified as belonging to Noon. Speaking for Noon, Captain Gotterel of *The Comus* said that Noon had been perfectly sober around seven o'clock on the evening of the fight. Gotterel however had gone back to the ship and had not seen Noon again. Then followed the eyewitness accounts and formal identifications of Noon being present in the *Le Gros Inn* when Thomas Hodge was killed. Advocate Godfray now requested more time to prepare his case which resulted in a fierce argument with the Procureur-General. The request was eventually granted and a second trial was ordered. Unsurprisingly, Noon was found guilty and he was then referred to a third and final trial, La Grande Enquête.

This third and final trial took place on 10 February 1846, in front of the Bailiff's representative, Edward Bisson (an Advocate) and seven Jurats plus a 'listening jury' composed of thirteen members. All the evidence and the witnesses were presented to the Court once again. Noon's defence was that he had not actually intended to kill Thomas Hodge. He simply struck him in a drunken rage because Hodge would not stop mithering him to tone down his language and had then attempted to escort him from the inn. This plea was entered in mitigation and consequently the jury found him guilty of manslaughter rather than murder. He was recommended for seven years transportation and confiscation of all his possessions. However, this decision had to be ratified by the Privy Council in England.

Two weeks later, on 25 February 1846, the Privy Council held a meeting at Buckingham Palace in front of Queen Victoria and His Royal Highness Prince Albert. Noon's case was on the agenda. The royal pair listened carefully to the details and to the conclusions of the trials held by the Royal Court in Jersey. Afterwards they conferred briefly and then Queen Victoria gave her decision:

> ... *John Noon to be transported out of the Island* [Jersey] *to Van Dieman's Land* [Australia], *or some one or other of the islands adjacent thereto, for the term of seven years. The period of his transportation to commence from the 10th day of February 1846* ...

What happened to John Noon afterwards is lost to history. Did he survive in the outback? Did he return in 1853 after his sentence had been served? Did he, as many did, build a new life for himself half a world away? The real question must be, though, is how and why John Noon could remain in denial for so long over a crime he committed in front of several eye witnesses all of whom could identify him beyond all possible doubt.

CHAPTER 21

Death of a Centenier
1846

Grabbing a carving knife ...
she drove it up to the hilt into
Le Cronier's stomach... 'O! mon
garçon!' he gasped. 'Je suis stabbé!'

n the nineteenth century St Helier was a busy port and the centre of a small but thriving ship building industry. While the town flourished and many undoubtedly prospered, there was, as in most ports, a seedier side of life. Sailors, who had been at sea and had not seen a woman for months or even years, had money to spend and appetites to satisfy. Once they had drunk their fill in the harbour-side taverns they started to look for a willing female with whom they could spend the rest of their night and often the rest of their money. Houses of 'ill repute', as they were, and are, quaintly called, did a brisk trade. There were several such establishments in St Helier and they were much in demand, though often fighting a running battle with the spoilsports of law and order whose aim in life, or so it seemed, was to close the places down and deprive the owners of a good living. The owners would argue, not without some justification, that it was safer and more comfortable for girls to entertain their clients in a house where there were other people around, but their pleas fell on deaf ears.

Patriotic Street was just off the main town centre of St Helier. Mulcaster Street ran parallel to it just off Mulberry Place. It was not the most select part of town but the visiting sailors didn't complain. They could get a good meal, a decent pint of beer, and what was then sometimes cheerfully called 'dessert', at reasonable prices. To them the so called 'houses of ill repute' were far from that description and offered them a few home comforts when they were often far from home. Marie Le Gendre kept one of these houses of ill repute at Mulberry Cottage on Patriotic Street. The house wasn't that large but she tried to make it welcoming to ensure that her clientèle would want to return. There was enough competition for trade and Marie was not about to lose out. Sometimes she wondered why people like herself were called 'a madam'. To her 'a madam' was a well-to-do lady who didn't need to work for her living like Marie did and who wasn't constantly harassed by the law when gentlemen called. As was usual, her neighbours had complained about the comings and goings and eventually, as Marie knew they would, the police arrived.

Today it was Centenier George Le Cronier who stood on Marie's doorstep. Her husband, who was pleased enough to live off Marie's share of the girls' earnings', always conveniently disappeared when he got wind of the fact that there might be trouble brewing and left Marie to face the consequences on her own. She knew of George Le Cronier. He'd been the one to bring that John Noon to justice (see Chapter 20). Now someone like Noon who went around stabbing his friends deserved all he got but she was just trying to make an honest living by giving people a little bit of pleasure in their lives.

The Centenier, accompanied by the Constable's Officer, knocked on her door. He had a warrant for the arrest of Marie and her husband. Though fearful, Marie, however, was not for being arrested. Why couldn't they just leave her alone and go after real criminals. She told him sharply to leave her house at once. George Le Cronier told her that she could either come quietly or he would use force. Either way he was arresting her. He moved towards her and Marie suddenly saw red. Grabbing a carving knife which was lying on the kitchen table, she drove it up to the hilt into Le Cronier's stomach. The Centenier collapsed to the ground with a cry, 'O! mon garçon! Je suis stabbé!' Marie had completely lost it now and, without care or ceremony, pulled the knife roughly out of his stomach and lunged again, this time at the horrified Constable's Officer. He, however, was too quick for her and rushed into the street shouting that his colleague had been murdered. Help was swift in coming and George Le Cronier was rushed to hospital. It was too late. He died the next morning with the distinction of having become the only Centenier in Jersey to be killed in the line of duty.

Marie Le Gendre was tried for murder by the Royal Court but she was spared the death penalty. Maybe the Royal Court felt that her absentee husband should have shared at least some of the blame. If he had stayed to support Marie then the consequences might not have been fatal. Perhaps some members of the Court knew Marie better than they should. As it was Marie was banished from Jersey for life. She was certainly lucky to escape being hanged for the wilful murder of a policeman. Years afterwards came the news that she had made a new life for herself and had remarried. By a freakily ironic coincidence her new married name was Mrs Le Cronier. One would have thought that she might just want to forget and that she would have persuaded her new husband to change their names; or maybe she never told him the truth about her background.

Today, Patriotic Street has changed beyond recognition. Marie Le Gendre's house is no longer standing nor are any of its neighbours. Instead, the street is dominated by a huge new carpark built on the site of a Red Cross depot from which food parcels were distributed during the Second World War. Marie's home must therefore have been destroyed at least almost seventy years ago and there is no trace of Mulberry Cottage in the surviving records. However, an adjacent road bears the name of Mulberry Street and perhaps the cottage, named after a long gone bush, stood close by.

While Marie had the burden of bearing the same name as the man she had killed, the town of St Helier ensured that George Le

Memorial tablet for Centenier George Le Cronier. The author

Cronier would never be forgotten by erecting a 25 ft tall (just under 8 m high) granite memorial to him in splendid Victorian Classical style. It stands at the southern end of Green Street Cemetery in St Helier, an ever present reminder of the man who holds a unique place in Jersey's criminal history.

The monument erected in memory of Centenier George Le Cronier. The author

CHAPTER 22

Poison Peas
1851

... it seemed that the pea soup was not up to its usual standard ... rather hard and seemed to have a slight taste of tobacco ...

The tragedy of this story is that neither Sherlock Holmes nor forensic science existed when it happened. It is the sort of case that Holmes would have relished. Moving from fantasy to fact, it is also the sort of case that forensic science would have solved quickly and accurately. As it was there was sufficient doubt as to who the real culprit actually was and as a result no one was charged, either at the time or since.

The Isabella was a Jersey ship captained by Francois Anley, a St Helier man. At the time of this story he was aged forty-two and married with seven children. He lived in the village of Longueville, not far from the old haunted Manor House. *The Isabella* had sailed from Lisbon on 25 February 1851. They had been at sea for ten days and were about fifty miles off Guernsey. It was a cold winter's evening and the Captain and his crew were looking forward to their dinner. The first course was pea soup, a Victorian favourite, and they ate gratefully, pleased to be having something warming. However, it seemed that the pea soup was not up to its usual standard and several of the crew commented that the peas were rather hard and seemed to have a slight taste of tobacco. Captain Anley sighed. He would have to reprimand the cook yet again. He had already reprimanded him on a number of occasions for his unhygienic habits. No doubt the wretch had dropped some of his pipe tobacco into the soup. As soon as the dinner was over he would go and have a word. He never got that far.

Almost as soon as he had finished his soup Captain Anley collapsed, clutching his stomach, and before the evening was over he was dead. His son, Francis, who was also on board working as an ordinary seaman, and several of the crew, were also violently ill and suffering severe stomach pains. Francis had in fact joked with the cook about there being tobacco in the soup and only ate a few mouthfuls which was why he did not die like his father, who had eaten heartily.

The decision was taken to try and reach *The Isabella*'s home port of St Helier, so that they could get medical help and give poor Captain Anley a decent burial. On Tuesday 12 March, *The Isabella*, its flags flying at half-mast, anchored off Jersey. A small boat put out and brought ashore the body of Captain Anley, and those crew members who were still sick; and took them all to the hospital in St Helier.

Two days later the *Jersey Times* reported that Captain Anley had not died a natural death. He and his crew had been poisoned with arsenic. The cook, Joseph Kingston, was arrested, and so was another member of the crew, Clement Miller. Neither had been seen to be ill. The cook had not eaten with the rest of the crew, and had stayed in his cabin after the fatal meal, and it had been Miller's turn to be at the helm during dinner so he did not eat any of the poisoned soup. Furthermore, Kingston gave evidence that Miller was in possession of arsenic. He was carrying it around with him, tied up in a piece of old stocking. However, Kingston said that he had not seen Miller go anywhere near the pot of pea soup.

Centenier Jean Chevalier was ordered to search the ship by the Constable of St Helier. A thorough search was made, particularly of the cabins and trunks of both Kingston and Miller. In Miller's trunk Chevalier found remains of arsenic hidden among his clothes. As a result of this discovery Kingston was discharged at the inquest on 15 March and the inquest jury sent Miller for trial, charged with 'wilful murder'. However, there was obviously some doubt about Miller's guilt. The whole case was just too pat and the inquest jury only decided to indict Miller on a six to five majority; that is, a majority of one. This obviously influenced the jury when the trial was held on Tuesday 18 April for they '... acquitted Miller and set him at liberty ...'

In the absence of other evidence or other suspects, no one else was charged. Most of the crew had been hired in London and did not seem to have either a history with Captain Anley or a grudge against him. Joseph Kingston, the cook, who did have a grudge against the captain, really was the obvious suspect but that does not explain why Clement Miller should have been carrying around quantities of arsenic with him. Did Kingston ask him to get it for him perhaps? Nothing seems to be known of the relationship between the two men. Were they old friends or just colleagues by chance? If Kingston was as innocent as he claimed to be, why and how did he know that Miller had arsenic in his possession, and why did he 'grass' on him? It would seem that the Royal Court proceedings left several very important questions unanswered.

CHAPTER 23

A Murder in St Peter
1866

*... she had fought hard for her life
and she had not died easily ...*

I t was a pleasant evening in early May 1866 in St Peter, a small village not far from St Helier. Just two days before there had been the May Day celebrations to celebrate the beginning of summer with its promise of long hot days and balmy nights. It was essentially a farming village and the old country customs were still practised with enthusiasm. The village worked on the agricultural calendar which meant that May was hailed as the beginning of summer. Early on the morning of May Day the young people would go 'a-maying' down to the woods to collect dew fresh flowers with which to decorate the maypole and the garments of the dancers around the maypole. It would be a general day of feasting and festivities and revelries to welcome the summer and the coming harvest. Great excitement was caused by the choosing of the May Queen and the girls of the village competed with enthusiasm. A May princess was also often chosen to attend the May Queen and the winners would ride like true royalty at the head of the May procession.

The May Queen that year was a pretty local girl and Esther Le Brun had enjoyed watching the procession of gaily decked flower carts, the pageantry of crowning the May Queen and the dancing around the maypole afterwards. Not that she had danced. Not now that she was old and her joints were stiff. She remembered the May Days of her youth when her parents were still alive and sighed nostalgically. Things had been so different back then. Esther Le Brun lived on her own in St Peter. She was lonely much of the time and she liked to join in all the events of her small community. It made her feel more a part of local life, as though she belonged somewhere. The excitement of all the May Day festivities, and the sewing she did, sitting on her green bed by the fire each evening, had made her tired and on the evening of 3 May she decided that she would have an early night. She might then spend the next day working in her garden if the weather was nice.

Joseph Bradley was a labourer but he preferred the easier way of making a living by burgling peoples' houses for he had discovered that crime really did pay. He'd worked out that people living alone might have more that was worth stealing since they wouldn't have family on whom to spend their money or lavish presents. His drinking funds were, as usual, running low, so bearing this piece of homespun wisdom in mind he began to look around and his eye fell upon Esther Le Brun's house. The old girl had been on her own for a while. She might have quite a little bit stashed away he thought. It was certainly worth a look and he wasn't worried about being caught. Even if she disturbed him she'd be no match for him.

Sometime during the night of 3/4 May, Bradley entered Esther Le Brun's house to look around and see what there was that was worth stealing but things began to go badly wrong. A noise wakened her and she sat up in bed just as he was going through the little drawers in her dressing table. She'd recognised him, of course she had, she'd seen him around St Peter often enough, which was awkward because there was one thing of which Francis Bradley was quite certain and that was that he was not going back to prison for burglary. She would have to be silenced.

St Peter's village where Esther Le Brun was murdered by Francis Bradley. The author

Esther Le Brun was found lying dead in her bed the next day. Bradley was an obvious suspect. It was, to use modern police jargon, his '*modus operandi*'. Added to which Bradley had escaped from prison on 14 April where he was being held for robberies. He knew the area and he'd been seen in the locality recently when he had been trying to hire a boat at Rozel on the preceding Friday to make his escape to France. It didn't take long to find Bradley and he was rearrested three days later on 7 May.

Bradley was charged with murder of Miss Esther Le Brun at St Peter by '. . . laying violent hands on her while she was in bed and suffocating her . . .' The trial was presided over by the Bailiff plus Jurats Le Gallais, Lerrier, Le Bailly, Le Quesne, Neel, Aubin, Marrett and Payn. The jury foreman was F J Le Couteur. It had been a brutal murder of a defenceless old lady and forty witnesses were sworn in. Advocat Vickery picked the short straw as the defence lawyer.

The prosecution described in bitter detail what had happened that night. Bradley had entered Miss Le Brun's house for burglary. She was 'an old and lonely woman' and he had suffocated her simply because she happened to be in the wrong place at the wrong time. She had fought hard for her life and she had not died easily. Dr Low described the posture of the body. He, Dr Le Cronier and Dr Godfray said that there were cuts on Bradley's hands and his clothes were bloodstained. Bradley tried to dismiss these facts and said he'd got the cuts when he was loading bricks on the quay but this proved to be just another lie of the many he told. Hearing the evidence of forty witnesses took some time and Bradley's case wasn't helped by the fact that he had boasted of previous burglaries and he had told his friend George Le Breton that he'd rather commit murder than fail in an attempt at robbery or do time for it.

The jury took only fifteen minutes to find him guilty and on Tuesday 10 July 1866 Francis Bradley was sentenced to death for the murder of Esther Le Brun. The Bailiff and the Jurats donned their customary black caps but Bradley was defiant, refusing to kneel for sentence to be passed, and had to be forced to his knees. He then swore obscenely at the Court and denied his guilt. Back in prison again Bradley was obstructive and vile mouthed and threatening. He persisted in regularly kicking the warders so he was shackled and handcuffed. At first he also refused any religious ministrations from either Reverend D Lampriere or Father Volckeryck of St Thomas RC Church. Bradley spoke little of his family; but he seemed cheerful enough and he certainly had a hearty appetite. One day he demanded a dozen eggs for breakfast and he was very miffed when he only got four. According to his jailer, J Le Rosignol, Bradley '... had omelette and coffee for breakfasts; chops or steak plus potatoes and salad for lunches, bread, butter and jam for tea (8.00 am; 1.00 pm; 6.00 pm) ...'

As was usual in these cases a plea for leniency was made and on 25 July 1866 a petition was sent to Queen Victoria asking for his execution to be transmuted to penal servitude for life or transportation. However, the petition attracted only a scant 350 signatures and no one of any note signed it which was also unusual. Finally, on Saturday 4 August the Home Office compromised and said it would agree to the terms of the petition if Royal Court approved. The Royal Court did not approve and the law took its course. Francis Bradley was hanged on Saturday 11 August at Gloucester Street in St Helier, still refusing to repent to the end.

It was a strange case in that Bradley seemed so cheerful about his impending exit from this world. It may, of course, have simply been bravado, but when people are putting 'a face' on it their true feelings usually make themselves known in other ways; like those of the notorious highwayman, Dick Turpin, who swaggered bravely onto the scaffold with a 'devil-may-care' attitude and his right leg shaking like a leaf. Not even he however managed to eat as heartily in prison like Bradley did. Appetite is usually the first victim of fear and stress. However, maybe life didn't have that much to offer Bradley in the first place or perhaps he just really didn't care. He died without either repentance or apology and maybe that was the way he wanted it.

CHAPTER 24

A Death in the Family
1875

'Is it possible that you think it is I who have done that?' he had asked in a whisper.

One of the strangest crimes in Jersey annals is that of a brother who was said to have murdered his sister in an appalling manner for no reason and then shot but not killed the only witness. As a result of not killing this witness, whose evidence appears to have been suspect because his account simply did not add up, the alleged murderer was sentenced to death and hung for a crime he maintained he never committed. It was a case which would have baffled the legendary Sherlock Holmes himself.

Joseph Le Brun, fifty-two years of age at the time of the murder, lived in St Lawrence near his sister, Nancy. Nancy Le Brun had been married for some years to a man named Philippe Laurens and they appeared to be reasonably content. Joseph and Nancy saw each other regularly and got on well together to all appearances. People who knew Joseph said that he had no grudge against his sister; in fact he seemed quite fond of her. He also seemed to be on amiable terms with his brother-in-law, Philippe. The three seemed to be part of just a normal agreeable family group.

Then, on a grey December afternoon, ten days before Christmas in 1874, the whole parish was shocked and saddened to learn that Nancy had been attacked in her home, and shot, several times, in the face, and then once in the head to make sure that she was absolutely dead; although that hardly seemed necessary under the circumstances. The murderer was then said to have fired the gun at Philippe Laurens, seriously wounding him in the leg and groin. This presumably was because Philippe was, or might be, a witness to the crime he had just committed. It didn't make sense. The

immediate question here was why did the murderer not kill
Philippe as well? Why would he allow the only witness of such a
terrible crime to live?

Philippe Laurens was found in a grievous state and taken to
hospital. He was still conscious and when asked who had done
this dreadful thing to him and Nancy he whispered painfully that
it had been Nancy's brother, Joseph. Folk were shocked. The
murder was a nasty one and people thought that it would surely
only have been committed by someone in a real passion of hatred
for the victim. Joseph Le Brun was simply not that sort of man
and besides he didn't hate the victim. She was his sister and he
loved her; or so it had seemed. Another problem was that Le
Brun had no motive for this killing. He and his sister had got on
well enough and he was not known to have any grudge against her
but Philippe Laurens was adamant. It had been Joseph Le Brun
who had pulled the trigger, killing Nancy and grievously wounding
himself.

The police were puzzled but treated him as a sincere and reliable
witness although he must have been in a state of severe shock when
he made the accusation. They lost little time in arresting Joseph
Le Brun but, apart from his brother-in-law's accusation, the only
evidence they could offer against Le Brun was his presence in the
locality of his sister's house. However, Joseph le Brun lived close
by, near Couvent and Villa, and there was no reason why he should
not have been near his home. Le Brun appeared to be very shocked
at being suspected of such a crime. 'Is it possible that you think it is
I who have done that?' he had asked, in a whisper.

This cut no ice with the police and he was arrested on Friday
17 December 1874, just two days after the murder. The evidence
however took three months (April to June 1875) to collect and
three hours to read to the court at the trial which began
Wednesday 7 July. The court was presided over by Bailiff Hammond and the Bench was composed of Jurats Lerrier, Marett,
Gruchy, Le Montais, Falle, Briard, Mourant and Le Gros plus the
Foreman Josue-Brayn. Advocate Westaway was defending Le
Brun. Despite the length of time spent collecting the evidence,
which was purely circumstantial, it was all over very quickly. It
seemed that the prosecution were very sure of their case and the
defence do not seem to have gone out of their way to point out the
flimsiness of a case built on such circumstantial evidence; although

Advocate Westaway felt that there was something wrong with this case, a missing link which no one had discovered.

The jury were out for just seventy minutes. They found Le Brun guilty of the attempted murder of his brother-in-law but they were divided over the question of the murder of his sister. The Bailiff then questioned each member of jury and finally announced that a 'sufficient number' believed Le Brun guilty, although they had recommended him to the mercy of the Sovereign. This plea seems to have been ignored for Le Brun was made to kneel down as the Bailiff and Jurats (in their black caps) sentenced him to death.

Joseph Le Brun could not believe that this was happening to him. He protested his innocence and swore that he could never have done such a thing to anyone, let alone his sister. A petition pleading for commutation of sentence to penal servitude was sent to the Home Secretary but it was to no avail. Despite the conviction on circumstantial evidence, the law took its inexorable course and this, which was the last public execution on Jersey, was carried out on Thursday 12 August 1875.

The day before his execution, however, Le Brun's brother-in-law, Philippe Laurens, came to see him. There were several witnesses to the strange conversation which took place as follows:

PL: 'Joe, I'm sorry to see you here.'

J Le B: 'And you still wish to say that it was I who did it?'

PL: 'Yes, I repeat, you murdered my wife, as you wished to murder me, and no one else but you did it.'

J Le B: 'You have proof of that?'

PL: 'I did not come here to argue with you. I forgive you, but I say that you committed the crime. Adieu!'

The truth is often stranger than fiction but what would the latter-day Jersey detective Bergerac (John Nettles) have made of such a conversation? What motivated Philippe Laurens to go to the prison where Le Brun was being held and engineer this strange exchange? It was as if he wanted ensure some point had been made. Why would Joseph Le Brun have left the sole eyewitness to such a killing alive if he had been guilty? Was it a 'crime passionel' of some kind? Had Le Brun found out perhaps that his sister had been cheating on her husband? It was a savagely gruesome killing to shoot a woman several times in her face. He did not attempt to shoot his brother-in-law in the same manner. Had the pair set it up between them and then the brother-in-law had seized his opportunity to be rid of Le Brun whom he perhaps felt might blackmail him at some future point? What had happened to the gun and who had owned it? As Westaway said in Le Brun's defence, there was definitely something missing in the chain of evidence.

CHAPTER 25

Not Caesar, Only Romeo
1880s

Georges Boulanger ... had an
Achilles heel. Her name was
Marguerite de Bonnemain and he
was desperately in love ...

The nineteenth century was a troubled century in Europe, especially for France. The 1800s had begun with the Napoleonic Wars culminating in the defeat, exile and eventual death of the legendary Frenchman who had visions of such grandeur that he had wanted to become Emperor not just of France but of the rest of Europe. The passion of Napoleon's private life was his Empress, Josephine. Josephine also had passions, so much so that the battle weary Emperor could not always meet her demands, thus giving rise to that well worn phrase 'not tonight, Josephine!' When he was finally recaptured by the English and imprisoned on the lonely Atlantic island of St Helena he entered an exile that must have been long and lonely without her. As the century drew to a close another military Frenchman found himself forced to live without the woman he loved and that was something he could not face. He could not endure the pain of separation and he turned out to be made of less sterner stuff than the great Emperor.

General Georges Boulanger was the French Minister of War during the later 1880s. France was still jittery after several political upheavals and the trauma of what came to be known in Europe as 'the Year of Revolutions'. There seemed to be political and social unrest everywhere. For the aristocracy in particular, memories still fresh with the cruelties of the French Revolution, the dreaded guillotine and the grimness of the Bastille, it was a time of great unease and they looked for a strong leader; someone who could ignore parliament and the politicians, take charge and exercise a firm control. Georges Boulanger seemed to be that man.

Maison du General Boulanger: General Boulanger's house in St Brelade c.1900.
Author's collection

As the new Minister of War in January 1886 the General was popular with everyone: the army, the aristocracy and the ordinary people. A man in whose capable hands the reins of power could be held easily. His first chance to seize power came on 2 December 1887, in the wake of a government scandal, but he was relaxing at a country inn with his mistress and either could not or would not return to Paris in time. Notwithstanding this, the Boulangist movement progressed steadily throughout 1888 and on 27 January 1889 Georges Boulanger was elected a Parisian Deputy by a large majority (over 250,000), and with such huge support he again seemed set fair to take over the power of government in France.

Hailed privately by some as the new Caesar, Georges Boulanger nevertheless had an Achilles heel. Her name was Marguerite de Bonnemain and he was desperately in love with her. She had been his mistress for some time and he delighted in her company. Wherever he went so did she and the reverse was also true. He could not bear to be without her. His enemies saw this weakness and realised that it might be their chance to rid themselves of him. General Boulanger and his followers were secretly plotting to overthrow the French government, although the General had some misgivings about a planned coup. He would then take charge and on the crest of his wave of popularity he would become virtual dictator of his country. Someone who should perhaps not have been privy to this plotting 'leaked' news of his plans. Just a few hours before the coup was due to take place charges were brought against Madame de Bonnemain by his political opponents.

If the lady had kept her head, so to speak, or rather her cool, she would have realised that these charges, of a vague nature, would not stick, and all she had to do was to sit tight and stick it out. Marguerite de Bonnemain, however, panicked. Terrified of being arrested she left Paris and fled to Brussels. Like the English King Edward VIII half a century later, General Boulanger could not countenance ruling his country without the woman he loved by his side, and, like Edward VIII, he too abandoned his responsibilities. He followed his love to Brussels immediately and the Boulanger movement collapsed almost at once. As one of his supporters complained bitterly '. . . we thought he was Caesar but he turned out to be only Romeo . . .'

Romeo and Juliet were not destined for a happy ending and nor were the General and his lady. They considered it wiser to leave the Continent and so they travelled to Jersey. Here they found a house in St Brelade for their love-nest which had been built in 1837 by an eccentric Parisian collector named Vanier. Château des Roches was a mixture of styles, both externally and internally, but it was pleasant and comfortable and overlooked the bay. For two years they lived here in tranquillity and happiness, dreaming of their return to France and plotting a fresh coup to overthrow the French government. However, it turned out that this was not to be the case.

Marguerite de Bonnemain became seriously ill. The General was frantic and paid for her to have special treatment in Brussels. It was no good. Despite every effort by her doctors she died early in September of 1891. The General was inconsolable. Somehow he got through her funeral but his grief overwhelmed him. Never to see her again. He could not stand it.

On 30 September 1891, a few days after Marguerite had been buried at Ixelles in Belgium, Georges Boulanger emerged briefly from his blur of tears and drink. He had come to a decision. Dressing himself in his smartest clothes he took his pistol from the cabinet in his study and went to the cemetery. There, standing by the grave of the woman he had loved more than life itself, he shot himself through the head. He collapsed onto her grave in much the same way as Romeo had collapsed when he learned of Juliet's death. Although the General had committed a 'crime' by committing suicide, it was widely accepted that he had done it out of love and he was allowed burial in the same grave as his precious Marguerite. It was a tragic resolution to a star crossed love story but the General was little mourned. As one of his former supporters drily remarked '. . . he lived as he died . . . always a second lieutenant . . .' Château des Roches still stands today but it has been converted into modern apartments and a luxury hotel, '. . . built for pleasure . . .', stands in the former grounds.

Hotel L'Horizon, *which stands in the former gardens of General Boulanger's house.* The author

CHAPTER 26

A Shocking Tragedy
1894

... he had been badly beaten and his features were unrecognisable ...

Three days before Christmas in 1894, John Francis, a young blacksmith who lived in St Ouen, decided to go for a festive drink. He was a tall, well built, muscular man of some twenty-nine years of age. Not yet married, or even engaged, he was considered a 'good catch' by many of the local girls. John was a man of sober habits, but Christmas was Christmas and there were goose raffles being held at the public houses down in Grève de Lecq. There was also a skittle alley at *The Prince of Wales* and John liked a game of skittles. When he arrived he met up with some of his friends, who included a married barber called Maletroit, a Frenchman named Ed Le Cornu, a tall fair haired sailor, and Henry Francis, one of his nephews. They played a few games of skittles and enjoyed a few drinks. As it was Christmas John drank sherry but he was moderate in the amount he consumed. When the landlady, Mrs Simon, called time at 11.00 pm, no one was drunk, she said, but there was a real party atmosphere in anticipation of the coming Yuletide celebrations. Soon afterwards, John put on his overcoat and his tweed cap and set off to walk back home.

About seven o'clock the next morning Mr Tanguey, who lived in a cottage at the top of L'Étacq Hill, opened his garden gate and practically fell over the inert form of a man. He called his wife and together they managed to get the man into the house and laid him on the green bed. He was very cold and his face and clothes were covered in blood. Gently, Mrs Tanguey sponged his face but he had been badly beaten and his features were unrecognisable. Shocked, Mr Tanguey hastily summoned the Constable of St Ouen's and a local doctor.

John Francis was still alive but delirious from his wounds. He rambled about his work in the forge and about his friends but he appeared unable to recognise some of those he knew well. Later that day Captain George Syvret arrived to question him, much to the distress of John's sister, Moira Francis. John, however, did recognise Captain Syvret, and he managed to tell him that he had been attacked by three men whom he thought had jumped from a trap and knocked him down. He did not know why. Robbery appeared not to be the motive since he still had his watch on him and four shillings and nine pence in his purse. There was little more he could add and his condition was worsening. Early on Christmas Eve John Francis died.

The local community was shocked. John Francis had been well liked and, so far as anyone knew, he had no enemies. Dr Falla and Dr Bentliff volunteered to work at David Place in St Helier on Christmas Day to carry out a post-mortem and establish how John Francis had died so that the inquest could be held on Boxing Day. The *Jersey Times* reported their findings in detail the following day:

> *... there were contusions 4 ins long by 3 ins wide on his forehead and over his eyelids and extensive haemorrhage in the surrounding tissues; contusions over the bridge of the nose and fracture of nasal bones; a small lacerated wound below his right eye; a slight injury to the right eye and the left eye had contusion. His upper lip was bruised against his teeth and his tongue slightly cut by his teeth. There was a contusion on his lower right cheek 3 ins long by 1½ ins wide. His skull was fractured; there was bleeding within the skull and extensive brain haemorrhage ...'*

Otherwise, the doctors stated, his organs were healthy and there were no other marks of violence on the body. Not unreasonably, the cause of death was given as 'head injuries'.

When he was attacked, John Francis had been smartly dressed in a collar and tie and a suit consisting of trousers, waistcoat and jacket. He was also wearing his dark overcoat and check tweed cap. In his pockets were his purse, his handkerchief and a tobacco pouch. He carried a heavy knobbed African thistle walking stick and it was obvious he had used this as he struggled violently to defend himself. John Francis had been the victim of a vicious and sustained assault that seemed completely motiveless.

The inquest opened at St Peter's Hotel at 3.00 pm on 26 December 1894. There were nineteen witnesses in attendance as well as the two doctors who performed the post-mortem, the Constable of St Ouen and two centeniers plus the Constable of St Helier and Centenier le Quesne. Pierre Ferchat of Cinq Verges in St Ouen officially testified, as did a number of witnesses, that John Francis had indeed played skittles with his friends on the Saturday evening and that they had all enjoyed a few drinks. John was in a happy mood and paying for his share of the drinks. All the witnesses agreed that no one was drunk although some were not sure who knew whom.

Walter Follien of Millars Vingaine said he passed St Peter's Church about 2.00 am, close to the spot where John Francis was found dying around 2.30 in the morning but he had seen and heard nothing untoward. His wife, Auguste Follien (née Mauger), had heard firm leisurely footsteps on L' Étacq Hill at about 5.45 am on the Sunday morning but she had not recognised them nor could she tell if they were going up or down the hill.

The jury was left with little option but to return a verdict that John Francis died as the result of a violent assault by a person or persons unknown. It turned out that the culprits were never found and brought to justice but a possible explanation of the killing was forthcoming.

John Francis did not take the quick way home that night. Instead he walked with his friends as far as Carrefour des Cinq Verges where Pierre Ferchat lived. Then he began to make his way home alone. Meanwhile, William John Cox, a cab driver, had taken a party of seven people from Broad Street St Helier to St Ouen. They had left St Helier at about 10.20 pm. He did not know six of them but he thought one might be a sailor. He had dropped them near the chapel in St Ouen before taking the last person, described as 'the bewhiskered Mr le Brun', whom he did know, to a destination further on.

Could these unknown people have been the ones who attacked John Francis? Yet surely Mr Cox would have recalled witnessing such an attack. John said two or three people had attacked him whereas Mr Cox had dropped six people in St Ouen. Of course they may have split up but then how or why did John believe that they had jumped from a trap? Perhaps there was another trap, unknown and unseen, which passed him, and whose occupants, for reasons unknown, chose to attack him. The case remains a 'shocking tragedy', as it was dubbed by the newspapers of the time, and a mystery whose solution has been lost to history.

CHAPTER 27

Bent Bluebottles
1894

PC Coutanche ... publicly fought with a woman ... he and PC Cahill had been seen frequenting the pubs late at night ... still on duty PC Noel had offered to procure young girls for those who wanted them ...

Police corruption is sadly nothing new. In recent years public faith in the men and women sworn to serve and protect the public from crime and criminals has been badly dented. Most police officers are decent law abiding citizens who try their best, but their efforts are besmirched by the few who betray their trust and give the police a bad name. Jersey, even though it is an island, had its share of corruption among its comparatively small force. The local police there were known as 'bluebottles' at the turn of the nineteenth century and it is from this nickname that the story takes its title.

During the early 1890s there was a spate of robberies from the inns and public houses of St Helier. Nothing was taken except bottles of liquor and at first the robberies were put down to local drunks and vagabonds. After a while however a more sinister pattern began to emerge. The *Jersey Evening Post* for 26 October 1894 carried a story of a robbery at the *Exeter Inn*, a three storey sturdy Georgian town house on Queen Street in the centre of St Helier. On the ground floor large double wooden doors on one side lead into a yard behind the building. The *Exeter Inn* is still a working public house and externally little has changed since this story took place.

Staff and family quarters were on the top floor of the house. The night of 25 October 1894 had been a busy one at the inn and the

The Exeter Inn, *Queen Street, St Helier, in 2007 but little has changed in over 100 years.* The author

task of getting folk to drink up after time had been called took quite a while. People wanted to tell one last story, have one last laugh, before they went out into the chilly autumn night. Glasses had to be washed and tables wiped before the staff could finally make their weary way to their own beds. The landlord took a nightcap with him as he climbed the stairs to his bedroom. He was very tired and felt that he had more than earned his tot of rum that night. All he wanted now was a good night's sleep but he was not about to get it.

At about 3.45 am Mrs H J Boyce, the landlord's wife and a light sleeper, was woken by a noise in her kitchen. She rubbed the sleep from her eyes and listened carefully. There was definitely someone moving about. Scared, she nudged her husband and whispered that there was someone downstairs. Mr Boyce struggled to open his eyes and raised himself on one elbow. He could see his wife's anxious face in the moonlight streaming through the window and by now he could hear the noises for himself. Grabbing an old walking stick which he kept in a corner of the wardrobe Mr Boyce crept downstairs and started to make his way towards the kitchen. He could see a dark form in the doorway at the end of the corridor and raised his stick ready to strike when the man turned around. Mr Boyce was startled to see PC Machon in the kitchen with PC Charles Coutanche waiting outside. PC Machon was not wearing uniform but it was not unusual at that time for policemen on Jersey to wear plain clothes when on duty.

PC Machon seemed unperturbed. He explained that he had found a window unlatched and, after trying in vain to knock Mr Boyce up, had entered the premises to search them, believing that the intruders were still inside. However, he had not found anyone. Mr Boyce trusted the police and he accepted the explanation without question. Later that morning he reported that six bottles of spirits were missing, lamenting the fact that the police had obviously arrived too late to apprehend the intruders. The two policemen reported to Sergeant Oldridge at St Helier police station that they had entered the *Exeter Inn* and their reasons for doing so. The next day, the case was taken before the court but the magistrate, John Vaudin, said he could see no case for dishonesty, maybe just an excess of zeal, and cleared PC Machon of any wrongdoing. Mr Boyce fitted new locks on his windows and no one thought anything more of the affair until a week later.

This time there was a similar occurrence at the *Navy Hotel* near the Town Church on the night of Hallowe'en. The hotel prided itself on its service, offering a grill room, hot and cold baths, and boasting that it was the only hotel on Jersey where grilled chops and steaks could be had at all hours. This may not have been quite true since when PC Machon was found inside the hotel around 1.30 am, claiming he had become suspicious about an open door, everyone was asleep. PC Noel was standing outside as though on guard. PC Machon again claimed that he had seen a window un-latched and he had entered the building to investigate the open door and window. This time the landlord, Mr Middleton, did not believe Machon's explanation and questioned his method of entry. Furthermore, said Mr Middleton, the sash of the window in question was weighted, and the window could not possibly have remained open. Machon now changed his story and said that he'd entered by the open front door and had relocked it. He was asked to give a description of the key but said that he could not remember what it had looked like. That, said Mr Middleton, was because the door had been bolted and barred. It had had no key for six months.

Twice in one week was a bit of a coincidence and then a local reporter uncovered yet another instance. The robbery at the *Exeter Inn* had taken place on 26 October; the *Navy Hotel* was entered by police in the early hours of Hallowe'en; and finally there was an incident at another unnamed hotel on 3 November whose land-lord, Mr Boniface, also did not believe the explanations given by the police for being inside his premises. This was beginning to look like too much of a coincidence and the *Jersey Times* reported these events together with a strongly worded attack on the local police force, talking of the '... manifest defects of our police system ...'

The police were naturally furious and Mr Baudains, the Con-stable (a sort of Chief Constable for the Island), wrote to the Attorney General, as a result of which the *Jersey Times* publisher, Philip Mourant de la Mare, was arrested on a charge of libel. This proved to be an unwise move. When the case came to court wit-nesses were called who testified that PC Machon was often drunk, their testimony corroborated by a local physician, Dr Voisin. PC Coutanche had publicly fought with a woman in Poohnah Road, St Helier. Both he and PC Cahill had been seen frequenting the pubs late at night (presumably still on duty). PC Noel had offered to procure young girls for those who wanted them and could pay; and yet another policeman had given what amounted to a guided tours of local brothels.

It was not an edifying spectacle and, of course, Mr de la Mare was found 'not guilty'. Indeed, there could hardly have been any other verdict. PC Machon was dismissed from the Force. PC

Coutanche was initially suspended and then dismissed for his fight with the woman in Poonah Road. PC Cahill was suspended for two months and another policeman was reprimanded for fighting in a public house. It was a sad indictment of the Jersey police and one which led to several reforms. The *Jersey Times* appointed itself as a kind of police watch dog and continued its vigilance for a number of years.

CHAPTER 28

It *was* an Accident
1894

... the tranquillity was shattered by the sound of a gunshot and a woman screaming ... Elizabeth Jane sank to the floor clutching her face ...

Eight o'clock in the evening on Monday 17 September 1894. It was a peaceful evening in early autumn for the residents of Trinity parish in the north of Jersey. The day was winding down and folk were seeking their own firesides. Kettles were set on hobs to boil and the women were looking forward to a good gossip while their men enjoyed a pint in the local pub. In her house at La Boucterie, Elizabeth Jane Mourant called to her husband to ask if he wanted a cup of tea from the pot she had just brewed. The next moment the tranquillity was shattered by the sound of a gunshot and a woman screaming; and Elizabeth Jane sank to the floor clutching her face.

Tea forgotten, her parents rushed to their daughter's side. Elizabeth Jane's face had been shattered by the shot and she was in the most agonising pain. Meanwhile, her husband had fled from the house and gone to the pub. Elizabeth Jane's parents staunched the wounds as well as they could and took her straight to the hospital. The next morning Dr Bentliff was called to the hospital by the Constable of Trinity to examine a patient who had been grievously injured. He arrived at lunchtime and there he found Elizabeth Jane Mourant in a pitiable state. Her face was covered in blood, her nose shattered and her teeth gone. Her tongue was perforated and her eyes were perforated with shot. He tended her wounds as best he could but two days afterwards her left eye became so inflamed that he had to remove it. Although Dr Bentliff believed that she would retain the sight in her right eye she would be dreadfully scarred for the rest of her life. He estimated that the gun had been fired into her face from a distance of 3 ft or less.

The Constable lost no time in arresting her husband, Francois Mourant. Mourant had already been placed under citizen's arrest and held in a local pub owned by his friend, George Dreland, to await the arrival of the Constable. He claimed in his defence that the shooting had been just a tragic accident and when he was asked why he had fled through the window immediately afterwards he said that he had panicked when he saw the state of Elizabeth Jane's face. Somewhat petulantly he went on to say that Elizabeth Jane and her mother had come home drunk again and he wanted to teach them a lesson, gain some respect from them. He hadn't meant for the gun to go off; he wasn't quite sure how it had happened, but in any case he maintained that he hadn't seen her standing there so close to him or he would have put the gun down. It was a strange defence and since Francois Mourant was not blind it would have been impossible for him not to have seen her standing there right next to him.

Francois Mourant lived with his wife, Elizabeth Jane, in his father-in-law's house. His friend, Dreland, claimed that, although Mourant was a model of sobriety, Elizabeth Jane drank and was always arriving home drunk. Elizabeth Jane claimed that simply was not true. On the night in question she'd arrived home and put the kettle on to boil for tea. When she turned to ask her husband if he wanted a cup of tea he shot her in the face. Her parents, who had witnessed the shooting, supported Elizabeth Jane's version of events. Her mother said that there had been no recent dispute between themselves and Mourant but he was an alcoholic who occasionally beat up his wife. He had failed to recognise that respect had to be earned and that it was not due as a given right.

Whatever the family disputes everyone was agreed that it had been a terrible thing to do and no woman deserved that to happen to her. Mourant's behaviour afterwards was nothing short of callous and strengthened the claims that he was addicted to the drink. No one was inclined to take his claims that it was an accident very seriously. Elizabeth Jane did not die but she was dreadfully disfigured and often in pain. Francois Mourant was remanded in gaol and sent for trial where he was eventually found guilty. The punishment does not seem to have been recorded, or if it was, it has been lost to history. One simply hopes that it was a punishment to fit the crime.

CHAPTER 29

Left to Starve
1900

... both were weak and emaciated
... almost dead of starvation.

There was a curious story in the *Chronique de Jersey* for Saturday 1 December 1900. Two ladies, one aged about forty-five-years-old, the other around seventy, were found lying wrapped in each others' arms on the floor of an almost empty house in St Helier. Both were weak and emaciated. The eyes of the older lady were sunken in her face and she could not even speak. They were almost dead of starvation. The son of the younger woman was found in a similar state in another room. Their family business had failed and their possessions had been sold the previous August by the local bailiff. Since then they had managed to buy food by selling their clothes, being too embarrassed and too highly principled to seek help from funds for the poor of the parish. They were sent at once to the local hospital (the English equivalent of the workhouse) just in time to save them from dying for want of food. The old lady's name was Mrs McGuire and the story behind their plight was heartbreaking.

Towards the end of 1898 an English gentleman named Luwee Harris had adopted a boy in Jersey who was her grandson. This was done with the full consent of the boy's parents, Mr and Mrs Maguire. At the time they were living in reduced circumstances owing to the recent failure of their business. Subsequently, the boy went to live with Mr Harris, taking his name. About two weeks after the adoption Mr Harris had the child baptised and several members of the boy's blood family were present. Luwee Harris was a prosperous professional man, who fed, clothed, and housed his adopted son generously, and sent him to the High School for Boys at Colomberie on Jersey. Mrs McGuire's grandson, who had not been well treated by his parents, appeared to be very content with his new circumstances. In July 1899, Mr Harris and his adopted son moved to England, preparatory to emigrating to Canada; but two months later, in September, the Maguires changed their mind and wanted the boy back. Mr Harris refused, whereupon the child was 'kidnapped' and taken to Guernsey where his parents, having moved away from Jersey to escape their problems, were now living.

Furious, Mr Harris lodged proceedings against the Maguires. However, on 22 October, the boy left his parents and returned to Mr Harris, whereupon the two of them sailed back to Weymouth. On arrival at the port the boy was detained by the Weymouth police and next morning Mr Harris and his adopted son appeared before the court in Weymouth. Here it was decided that in a case such as this one neither the police nor the local justices of the peace had any right to detain either Harris or the boy and both were released. Mr Harris now wanted his custody rights to be settled in the English High Court and so he and his adopted son remained in Weymouth to await the arrival of Mr Maguire. However, when Mr Maguire arrived he did not institute any legal proceedings but made another attempt to kidnap the child which was foiled by the Weymouth police. Mr Maguire then insisted a warrant be issued on Guernsey for Mr Harris's arrest.

The warrant was issued. Mr Harris was arrested and Mr McGuire got his unwilling son back. McGuire had left his mother, sister and nephew to fend for themselves when he moved to Guernsey to try and recover, by fair means or foul, the son he had given up for adoption. This was not the frantic search of a bereft father whose son had been taken at birth; but the act of a cruel and calculating man. Mr Maguire, who was very economical with his version of events, insisted on the arrest and charging of Luwee Harris because he had not willingly given up his lawfully adopted son. As a result Mr Harris was tried, found guilty (to the amazement of most islanders) and imprisoned, while the unfortunate boy was forced to return to his natural parents. In order to achieve this, Mr Maguire had been willing to sacrifice his own mother and sister, and leave them to starve to death on Jersey.

Chapter 30

Murder in a Cornfield
1906

Edouard didn't notice the body until he practically fell over it . . .

July of 1906 was a hot and sticky month on Jersey. Fields of yellow corn, ripe for cutting, drooped their heads, sometimes nodding to each other in desultory fashion if there was a gentle breeze. Soon it would be harvest time and as Edouard Le Cornu tramped through one of the these cornfields, which belonged to Swans Farm near St Saviours Rectory, on Thursday 19 July that year, he was thinking about how everyone would be gathering together soon to help cut the corn. His neighbours always helped him and he in turn helped them. After the harvest was gathered in he looked forward to the harvest supper and the dance that would follow it. Edouard was hot and thirsty. He knew he should have gone round the edge of the field but that would have taken him much longer. Although it was only eleven o'clock in the morning the sun was high. It was very warm and there was little breeze. His mind on the harvest, Edouard didn't notice the body until he practically fell over it.

Pierre Le Guen lay on his back in a pool of blood with his trousers half down and he wore no boots. He had been beaten to death. Edouard crossed himself and went at once to fetch help. When the police arrived Edouard found himself in the way so, while they examined the body, Edouard and his son, Albert, decided to help by searching the area. Bergerac would have deplored such an action but this was 1906 and forensic science was a thing of the future. Albert and Edouard's search proved to be fruitful. They found two pieces of a fancy watch chain dotted with red beads, a belt smeared with blood, a straw hat, a lemonade bottle, and a stone covered in blood. The items lay about 5 ft (1.7 m) from the body across a dusty cart track. There were signs

The cornfield adjacent to St Saviours Rectory where Pierre Le Guen was found murdered in 1906. The author

of a severe struggle and spots of blood on the surrounding wheat and on the cart track.

Edouard and Albert Le Cornu, who lived on a farm adjacent to the corn field, said they had not seen or heard anything or anyone suspicious but the night before (Wednesday 18 July) Albert had been in the barn tending a sick cow and heard the farm dogs barking at around 1.15 and 2.15 am. At the time he'd not thought much of it, being more concerned with the cow. However, Le Guen had been dead for some hours when he was found and it was decided that the murder could well have taken place around the time the dogs were barking.

Pierre Le Guen was identified by his wife, Marie, although she said that the watch chain did not belong to him. He had been a man of stocky build, about 5 ft 6 in tall with a wide forehead and tousled hair. He had a droopy moustache after the fashion of the time and slightly protruding teeth. If Marie was to be believed he also had a temper and a violent side to him. Marie said that he used to beat her regularly. As a result they were estranged and living apart at the time of his death. This being the case she really could not be expected to know his movements nor the people with whom he had associated since he left home.

On the face of it the police decided that this crime appeared to be a simple case of a man being killed by a person or persons as yet unknown following some sordid little squabble which had got out of hand. Pierre Le Guen was not known to have had any particular enemies and robbery did not seem to have been the motive. It was a mundane case which would be solved in due course, they felt, by solid plodding police work. However, it turned out to be anything but mundane.

Dr Charles Albert Bois carried out post-mortem on Pierre Le Guen two days after Le Guen's death and part of his report was published in the local paper:

> ... *witness* [Dr Bois] *recognised the skull as belonging to the body of Pierre Le Guen. The piece of bone detached from the skull was partly fractured previous to the post-mortem examination, and finally quite separated at the post mortem by having to be sawed through. The injuries had every appearance of being caused by a blunt instrument* ... *witness* [Dr Bois] *also saw a bloodstained stone* ... *from the attitude of the body and from the trampled wheat in the field, it appeared that there had been a struggle* ... *the more salient features are the long fractures on each side of the head and the fact of there being about two ounces of extravasated blood on the left side of the brain surface between the brain and the dura matter; also the large number of incised and lacerated wounds on the external surface of the head* ...

He added that Le Guen had been beaten to death in an attack '... with a rock 7 ins long by 5 ins wide which had same blood group on it as dead man and same hair ...' which matched the description of the bloodied stone found by Edouard and Albert Le Cornu. Dr Bois then concluded:

> ... *the cause of death was shock and haemorrhage due to the severe injuries to the head. From the appearance of the injuries, witness* [Dr Bois] *was able to come to the conclusion that they could not have been self inflicted* ...

Dr Falla, who had helped with post-mortem, gave further details:

> ... *the right arm was fixed in a position of self defence. Post-mortem rigidity was well marked, and it was nearly impossible to bend the*

*limbs. There were several pools of coagulated blood on the cart track
and some trampled wheat opposite the body . . .*

But incredibly, he suggested that the death could have been a
suicide (one suicide took place around every three weeks on
average at this time). However, suicides do not usually beat themselves to death by bashing in their head with a stone and Le Guen's
injuries were so severe it really was quite out of the question in this
case.

The watch-chain pieces found near the body came from a fob
watch and Mrs Le Guen was adamant that they did not belong to
her husband. Another piece of the chain had been found on the
cart track which led into the field by a local gardener, George
Martin. The inquest had concluded, in spite of Dr Falla's sug-
gestion, that there had been some sort of struggle as a result of
which Le Guen had been killed. So began the long process of
trying to piece together what had happened to the unfortunate
Pierre Le Guen.

François Poulain (a friend who had also identified Le Guen's
body) had seen the deceased at 12.30 pm, on Tuesday 17 July
when Le Guen had been in the company of his brother-in-law,
Thomas Connan. Poulain had seen him again at 1.45 pm that day
and they had gone together to St John, a tiny northern parish some
four or five miles from St Helier, looking for farm work. The two
had returned to St Helier at about 10.00 pm, having stopped en
route to relieve their thirst in the local hostelries. By about
11.20 pm they were in Bath Street and by then Le Guen was
drunk. The last Poulain saw of his friend was around 11.30 pm
when Le Guen was eating some fried potatoes.

Mrs Amelia Macnamara said she had seen two men, both drunk,
in de Carteret Street about 11.20 pm. She had recognised one of
them as Pierre Le Guen from a photograph of the murdered man
which appeared in the *Evening Post*. He was wearing a straw hat.

Mr Yves Tourment was in French Quarter at 10.30 pm on the
17th when he saw Le Guen and Poulain together. About half an
hour later he saw Le Guen drunk in Bath Street and then again at
approximately 11.30 pm in company with a man whom he did not
know.

Mrs Françoise Arzul, a friend of Marie Le Guen, had said that
Pierre Le Guen and Thomas Connan were good friends and drinking partners and that Connan might have been the man whom

Yves Tourment had seen with Le Guen. However, Marie Le Guen maintained that she and her brother, Thomas Connan, had gone to bed in her cottage at Le Bourg in St Clement about 10.00 pm, a fact verified by Mrs Josephine Couillard, a widow, who lived in the same house and had seen them both several times between 8.00 pm and 9.00 pm. Mrs Couillard was a light sleeper so she was sure that she would have heard any noise; especially occasioned through a struggle or by someone who was drunk.

PC Jouan, who was working on the case, knew that Marie Le Guen was estranged from her husband and had been able to tell them little about his movements, yet her brother, who lived in the same house, seemed to have been on very good terms with her husband and to have gone drinking with him regularly. Something was wrong somewhere but he could not put his finger on it. Acting on a hunch, he arranged to meet with Françoise Arzul in Peter Street, nearly three weeks after murder. He told her firmly that he thought she knew much more than she was saying and that if she did not tell him the full truth she could be an accessory to the crime.

Françoise was frightened now and finally she agreed to show PC Jouan a watch she had hidden in her cellar which belonged to Thomas Connan. She had lent Connan money on the value of the watch on Monday 16 July. She had noticed the pieces of watch-chain at the inquest and had thought they were like the watch-chain Connan had which she thought he had bought at Le Neindre's Jewellers in Hilgrove Street. Mrs Arzul then went on to say that she'd met Thomas Connan and Pierre Le Guen on 16 July near the Eastern Railway terminus. They all had a meal and a drink and she paid for it all. The two men had talked about how quickly Mrs Le Guen could spend money. Soon after this she had advanced him a loan of three shillings on the watch. Mid afternoon on Tuesday 17 July she had again met Connan and Le Guen walking near Town Church and they all went for a drink at the *Bunch of Grapes* which she paid for. Afterwards she left and the men had continued to get quietly drunk before leaving.

That night (of Tuesday 17 July), sometime after 10.30 pm, Françoise was woken by a knocking at her door. It was Connan wanting more money. She said she had none but gave him some bread. Connan smiled and said he'd be back later to stay the night. For some reason Françoise was frightened of him so she

'... [packed] her stockings in a basket, locked up her house, and spent the remainder of the night at a friend's nearby ...'

While Connan was at her house Françoise said she'd noticed a shadowy figure waiting in the street with a hat pulled down over the face. She had thought it was a woman but could not recognise her. When she left her house the street had been empty; but later that night she was sure she had seen (from the friend's house) two men and a woman walking towards College Hill. It was a strange story she told and was directly at odds with the evidence given by Poulain.

Jouan decided to investigate further. He learned that, three days before the murder, on 14 July, Thomas Connan had gone to see his previous employer, Mr Romeril, at Bel Royal, about getting his old job back. Mr Romeril had refused but the two had parted amicably enough. However, Romeril's daughters, ten-year-old Lilia and twelve-year-old Ethel, had noticed the fob watch and chain in Connan's pocket. '... you remember, mother,' Lilia said, 'that nice little chain with red beetles and black spots ...'

It was enough. Thomas Connan was arrested at Mr Gabent's shop in Bath Street. He was some twenty-seven years of age, with '... brooding deep set eyes, a thick bristly moustache and his short hair had a widow's peak over his wide forehead ...' Connan was bullish and surly and at first he denied owning a thirty shilling watch. How could he afford it? But then it was remembered that Pierre Le Guen had come into a little money and had given Thomas Connan some of it. Faced with the evidence Connan finally confessed.

His first words were that he was not alone in this affair. His sister, Marie Françoise Le Guen, was also involved. She had wanted her freedom from Pierre and had asked him to kill her husband. She in fact had dealt the first blow. Connan had walked into town; Marie had taken the last train. Connan had seen Le Guen eating his fried potatoes, and taken him to the railway station where they met Marie. The three of them walked towards the College, but, near St Saviours Church, Marie had led her husband into a corn field, and, pretending feelings she did not have, suggested they lay down together. Le Guen however passed out as a result of the amount of alcohol he had had to drink. As soon as he was asleep Marie had struck the first blow. Connan had then finished him off with his belt and removed Le Guen's boots.

St Saviours Rectory near the 'murder field' where the actress and society beauty Lillie Langtry was born and spent her childhood. The author

Marie Le Guen was arrested by Centenier P V Cooke of St Saviours. At first she had denied everything as well. Her brother had gone out about 10.00 pm on 17 July with his fishing knife and returned just after 8.00 am next morning, covered in blood and wearing her husband's boots. She had fainted with shock and horror. When she came round she was lying on the green bed and Thomas gave her some water to drink. Then he told her what he had done. She was appalled, she said, but she resolved to keep quiet for her brother's sake. He was family after all and her husband was dead. Nothing would bring Pierre back.

The case began to take on soap opera qualities however when Françoise Arzul told police of conversations she'd had with Marie and a Mrs Mattré who lived in St Mary at around 2.30 pm and 7.00 pm on the 17th to the effect that Marie would not divorce her husband as advised by her mother because she'd been told by a fortune teller that he would die quite soon anyway. Marie had said that her brother was angry with Pierre because he'd been 'bad-mouthing' her and drinking heavily. She then suggested that Mrs Mattré might like to go with Connan and 'hit' Le Guen and that if she would do so Marie would give her thirty shillings. Mrs Mattré had reluctantly confirmed this conversation although she'd refused to take up the offer. Even more amazingly the conversations had been heard and already reported by one of the island 'tattle-tale' gossips, a Mrs Marguerite Sequillon.

A further detailed search of Marie's home revealed a pair of elastic boots very similar to those Pierre Le Guen had worn; a bloodstained petticoat dress of Marie's; and a purse with a tear in the pocket also very similar to that owned by Le Guen. Connan was alleged to have swopped his own boots for Le Guen's. This allegation was confirmed by the discovery of a pair of boots by Vigntenier Buesnel of St Saviours in one of his fields near the Hougue Bie. He had thrown them across the road; one landing at Broadlands, the other at the foot of the Princes Tower (which formerly stood on the Hougue Bie). He'd retrieved them after hearing of the murder and its circumstances. Although Marie still refused to admit to anything the brother and sister were charged and sent for trial. Advocate Le Gros was retained to defend Connan and Advocate Richardson defended Marie.

Nothing about this case was to prove simple. Marie Le Guen was in service and she had a room at Le Bourg in St Clement. She also picked potatoes for Mr Couillard at Marais in Grouville and said that her husband used to beat her when he was drunk (which was quite often); and he also used to threaten her and keep her short of cash. As a result of the treatment he meted out to her, she said, they had separated two years ago. Centenier Labey had bound Le Guen to keep the peace in July 1905 after he had threat-ened to hang his wife. However, the *Jersey Evening Post* stated that Le Guen was a very mild mannered man!

There were certainly at least two sides to Pierre Le Guen. Mrs Marie Rose Vigué stated that Pierre Le Guen had come to her public house with a young girl on the Friday before his death. They had a meal and he'd paid for it with a sovereign from a purse which had contained ten or twelve sovereigns. She identified the purse shown her by Centenier Le Quesne as Le Guen's by the broken catch. After their meal Le Guen had asked her where he could get a room for himself and the girl and she had told him. Mrs Vigué's story appeared to be confirmed by the presence of a number of young girls in the public gallery throughout the trial. She'd seen Le Guen, a quiet man she said, many times during the last year but not his wife. The previous year both Pierre and Marie Le Guen had eaten together in her pub during the potato picking season. Marie had told Mrs Vigué she was picking potatoes to earn money because Le Guen kept her short of cash.

A receipt and guarantee from Emile Hyacinthe La Niendre was produced for a silver watch no 30358 and two chains (plated and nickel) bought from him on 5 July 1906 by Thomas Connan. Connan's full name was Thomas Joseph Connan and Emile remembered the receipt because he'd made a mistake and made it out to Joseph Connan and not Thomas Connan. The chains were those remembered by the little Romeril girls. Although Connan had excellent character references from the Mayor of St Malo, previous employers and those who knew him in his Brittany home town of Ploezal, Côtes du Nord; and was also said to have been a kind and attentive son to his parents; possibly the main influence on the jury was the exhibit of Le Guen's head, hacked off at the neck. This was in pre-forensic science days and they had already seen the weapon and scene of crime.

The trial lasted five days. Despite witness discrepancies and Marie's story of a violent and horrendous marriage; it took the jury just two hours on Friday, 11 January 1907, to deliver a guilty of murder verdict against Thomas Connan and Marie Le Guen; but they recommended the clemency of the court only for Connan. Bailiff Sir W H Venables Vernon sentenced Connan to death and Marie to twenty years penal servitude. Feelings ran high. Many felt that it was Marie who deserved to die.

A petition was sent to King Edward VII. He consulted the Home Office who rejected the plea. The law on public executions had not changed since Le Brun's time in August 1875 so a special law was rushed through. On 16 February 1907 public executions were banned in Jersey and on 19 February Thomas Connan was hanged at the gallows on Gloucester Street/Patriotic Street where today a large car park stands. When he finally knew that there was no hope for him Thomas Connan sat and wrote a confession in which he stated that he alone was responsible for the murder of Pierre le Guen but that it was at the instigation of his sister who desperately wanted her liberty. Marie had not been with him that night but had been, as she'd said, in her own bed.

It was probably a more likely scenario than the spectacle of them both climbing silently out of the cottage window in St Clement and taking tortuous separate routes to guide Pierre Le Guen to his fatal meeting. Marie had obviously been desperate to escape an abusive and violent marriage. She knew that her husband liked his drink and she must also have known of his predilection for young girls. Islands are small places when it comes to gossip. Her crime was not to go through the legal channels. However, in 1906 these would have been expensive and difficult indeed, especially for a woman. There was no such thing as legal aid and she lived in an age where society saw nothing particularly wrong with a husband beating his wife. There is little doubt that she turned to her brother for help and quite possibly she agreed with his solution to the problem. It was a decision for which both of them paid dearly.

CHAPTER 31

Foul Deeds and Tragedies of the Occupation
1940–45

... the Islands were just another stage in their journey towards death ...

I t is difficult for those on the UK mainland to understand what the Channel Islands went through in 1940. England has not been conquered or occupied for a thousand years since William the Conqueror sailed across the Channel from Normandy. It has been a 'free country' for longer than most countries in the world today. Since the days of King John the Channel Islands have looked to England for protection. Protection is what they received during the eighteenth and nineteenth centuries when the French were causing a lot of problems. However with the German advance and aggression of the mid twentieth century it was a very different story. Jersey shares the same status as Gibraltar. It is a Crown Dependency. That is it is dependent on the English monarch for protection. In the Second World War Gibraltar was both evacuated and defended. The Channel Islands were only partly evacuated, mostly due to misinformation and disorganisation on the part of both the Channel Island and English authorities. Then, far from being defended, the Islands were quickly demilitarised and left to their fate.

The Channel Islands were very vulnerable to German attack and the idea was to try and lessen possible civilian casualties. This ploy might have worked if someone in Whitehall had remembered to tell the Germans that the Islands were unarmed, undefended and would offer no resistance. No one did, so when the German planes flew over Jersey and Guernsey and saw lorries on the quaysides they assumed that the lorries were troop carriers and bombed them. In fact the vehicles were trucks unloading potatoes for export. The raid seemed to last forever but in reality it was only a

Loading potatoes at St Helier harbour, c.1920. Author's collection

few minutes. When it was over pieces of metal, smashed up trucks and bodies lying in a mush of blood and crushed vegetables, littered the quaysides. Then the Channel Islands knew that they were at war.

Jersey suffered patiently along with the other Channel Islands in the five year occupation by the Nazis during the Second World War but they had strong competent leadership from their Bailiff, Alexander Coutanche. He has been much criticised for not insisting on evacuation for more Jerseymen and women but initially he did not believe that the War would last for such a long time nor that the Occupation would be as prolonged and as miserable as it turned out to be. However, he stood his ground as far as he could with the German commanders and negotiated with them to gain the islanders concessions; often successfully interceding on behalf of those who were accused of some misdemeanour and threatened with transportation to concentration camps on the continent. When the Germans issued public orders Coutanche, on the pretext of obeying them, dragged his heels as much as possible, pleading one delay after another to the Germans. As a result minor ones often got overlooked and were sometimes not carried out.

This overlooking however was never going to happen with those orders regarding the Jews. Such orders came from the Führer himself and simply could not be disobeyed. No German officer would or could dare to cross the Führer. Alexander Coutanche, at some considerable personal risk, told German officers that the singling out of Jewish people for registration and restrictions was wrong and he was loath to do it. He was sharply reprimanded and told that he was to do at once what he was ordered to do. Had he been a person of lesser profile he might well have been sent to a concentration camp himself for daring to suggest such defiance but the Führer had ordered a 'model occupation' of the Channel Islands and imprisoning a local and well liked Bailiff would have been neither good policy nor good publicity.

Alexander Coutanche deployed his usual delaying tactics but eventually even he and Jersey had to toe the line on the Jewish question. His stance however had not gone unnoticed by Jersey people and many followed his example by appearing to be acquiescent to their German overlords while quietly defying them as much as they dared. Care was needed for Jersey, like Guernsey and Alderney, is an island, and if they were caught there was nowhere to run. The Führer had already announced that for every crime against a German on Jersey ten islanders would be punished and Jersey folk were frightened for their family and friends. Nevertheless, one Jewish girl, who faked her own suicide in 1943, was successfully hidden in St Helier by Jersey islanders until the war was over. Such was the secrecy that even to this day the identity of those who gave her shelter and saved her life is not known, at least in the public domain.

There is no doubt that people on Jersey suffered a great deal during the later years of the Occupation. At the beginning food was still in good supply, but, as rationing came in and shortages in certain foodstuffs began to appear, a black market grew and flourished. There are excellent descriptions of black market goods and trading practices given in *Jersey under the Jackboot* (R C F Maugham, 1946). The truly horrifying thing was that the black market was mostly run by Jersey people who made small fortunes out of their Jersey neighbours' deprivations. Maugham tries hard to defend some of his countrymen's actions but even he has to admit a few went too far and quotes examples of foodstuffs being stolen from shops and public storage depots, thus creating shortages, and then being sold on to the public at ridiculously inflated prices by the marketeers.

How could this happen within a small island community which should have faced the hardships together and created a strong community spirit? Part of the answer may lie in reading between the lines of Maugham's book. He expresses outrage at the disappearance of commodities such as sugar and jam; he bemoans the introduction of rationing; he is horrified to learn that nettles are being eaten in place of spinach and he is shocked to discover that people are using wooden footwear.

Part of Jersey's problem may have been that until World War Two the island simply had little idea of what really harsh deprivation could mean. For example jam was an unheard of luxury to the millions of workers who toiled in the dark satanic factories of the millscapes in nineteenth century northern England. The daily diet of the poorest (and they were in their tens of thousands) for most of their lives was onion porridge (provided by the mills for the child workers); bread and dripping, potatoes, and sometimes, a real treat was to boil up the bodies of miscarried calves. Most mill workers routinely wore wooden clogs until the 1960s and they were also known to boil stinging nettles as a substitute for spinach until the same date. Even today nettle soup is still made in many parts of the UK.

The food situation continued to worsen and finally, as the Allies gained ground, a number of basic foodstuffs became unobtainable. Food imports became scarcer until even bread was severely rationed. Eventually, in 1944, Churchill refused to allow any supplies at all to reach the Islands in order to starve out the Germans. Of course this move affected everyone and by 1945 the whole island was at starvation point. Churchill's strategy had backfired and reluctantly he finally agreed to allow the Red Cross supply ships through. For some it was only just in time.

One of the saddest stories to come out of wartime Jersey is that of Louisa Gould. She was born in 1891 and her two sons were grown up by the time of the Occupation. They had both enlisted to fight the Nazis and she missed them quite desperately. In 1941 one of her sons was killed and Louisa Gould was absolutely devastated.

It brought home to her the dreadful reality that all mothers faced in wartime. Mrs Gould was a kindly gentle soul who helped people whenever she could and it was mainly for this reason that she had given shelter to an escaped Russian prisoner. Bill Buryiv was a slave worker (see Chapter 31) who had escaped in 1943 and he was in a dreadful state for the Germans had a particular loathing of the Russians and treated them extremely badly. Louisa Gould knew very well what the penalty was for helping such a person but she said simply, 'I have to do something for another woman's son' and in so doing she signed her own death warrant.

Buryiv spent a year in hiding at Mrs Gould's house and then, unbelievably, she was betrayed to the Germans by a neighbour. A local doctor, John Lewis, condemned the betrayer as 'mentally sick' in his book *A Doctor's Occupation*, but it is far more likely that he or she betrayed Louisa Gould for a discreet cash handout or a few extra rations; or simply as a result of the 'tattle-tale' culture which existed in the Channel Islands at that time. The most famous example of this occurred on Sark in 1943 when an islander nailed a list to a tree on the main street naming all Sarkese who still possessed a radio set in direct contravention of German orders. The local German Kommandant was so shocked by such a blatant act of treachery that he tore down the list and refused to act upon it.

Mrs Gould was not so lucky. She and her brother, Mr Le Druillenecq, who was headmaster of St John's School, were arrested, tried and sentenced to two years in prison. On 1 July 1944 they were sent to France and by August of that year he was imprisoned in Belsen while she was sent to Ravensbrück. Louisa Gould was not sentenced to death and she should not have died, but she was worn out by grief and worry and her endless concern for others and she was by now in her mid fifties. She tried and failed to keep up with the punishing work schedule set by the Germans for prisoners in their camps. The Germans had no use and no time for those who could not work and on 13 February 1945 Louisa Gould was killed in the gas chambers of Ravensbrück. Her brother somehow survived the horrors of Belsen and he returned to Jersey heartbroken over the loss of his sister.

One of Louisa Gould's final acts of compassion had taken place on the long fraught journey to the concentration camps in open trucks. A Jersey man and his sixteen-year-old son travelled with them. The boy had been arrested for having a gun which had been

Eyewitness account of German brutality during the occupation of 1940–45. This incident occurred in St Ouens on 20 February 1943. The author

John Dalmau was a Spanish republican prisoner of war who witnessed horrific incidents of German brutality during the occupation of 1940–45 and wrote about them after the war. He remained on Jersey for the rest of his life. The author

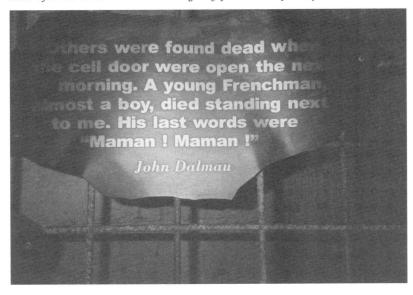

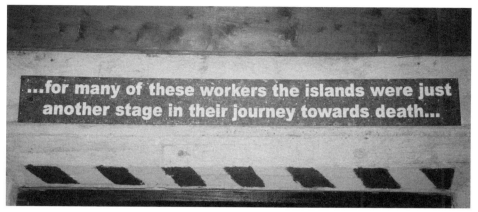

Entrance to commemorative museum for slave workers during the German occupation, 1940–45: Hougue Bie. The author

given to him long before the War and which he had never used. His father was arrested as an accessory. During the course of the journey the boy became seriously ill. Mrs Gould cared for him as best she could but without food, warmth and medicine she could not save his life and he died lying with his head in her lap as she softly stroked his face. The boy's father, weakened, disheartened and grieving, died in a German concentration camp soon afterwards.

This father and son were not alone in their fate. Dick Ogier, another Jersey man, was arrested for being in possession of a marked ordnance map. His father, a local lawyer, Advocate Ogier, was arrested for giving his 'criminal' son shelter and for not betraying him to the local German Kommandant. They were both sent to a French concentration camp. Advocate Ogier died soon afterwards. His son, Dick, survived, but died shortly after liberation and his return to Jersey.

There are a number of searing eyewitness accounts that have survived of the brutal and horrifying treatment to which forced labour prisoners, particularly Russian and Spanish workers, were subjected on Jersey during the Occupation:

> *... others were found dead when the cell door was opened the next morning ... a young Frenchman died standing next to me ... his last words were 'Maman! Maman!* ... (John Dalmau, Spanish PoW, 1944)

... one of those Russian workers was hanging by his feet and he was still wriggling a bit ... (Jersey Police, 1943)

... a Russian was in the pillory at Morville, St Ouens, with two branches of trees tied tightly round his neck and attached to two trees, the man just able to touch the ground with his toes ... (Edward le Quesne, 20 February 1943)

Jersey has commemorated the sufferings of its forced labourers and POWs by devoting a former German bunker at La Hougue Bie to their stories. The bunker is:

... dedicated to the thousands forced to labour for their persecutors 1940–1945 ... for many of these workers the Islands were just another stage in their journey towards death ...

There is also a 2 m high memorial of known graves and public acknowledgement of the unknown thousands '... who also served ...' To read their stories and to understand what they went

Sculpture created by Maurice Bilk, a survivor of Belsen, depicting the agony and suffering of slave workers during the German occupation, 1940–45. It stands at the centre of the Hougue Bie Memorial Centre. The author

'Liberation Sculpture', Liberation Square, St Helier, depicting (from left to right): Jersey couple from the Second World War; a member of the liberation forces; Jersey farmer and his family; all are holding aloft a Union Jack flag. The author

Bust and commemorative plaque in Royal Square, Jersey, for Alexander Coutanche, the Bailiff who led Jersey through the German occupation, 1940–45. The author

through is a truly humbling experience. In a way they were the foulest of deeds because they were committed so very impersonally by those in charge upon people they had never met or of whom they had no personal knowledge. In all the other stories in this book one person bears a grudge, has a motive, or is simply jealous or envious of another person. There is some connection between the victim and the criminal. In occupied Jersey that was rarely the case.

CHAPTER 32

Deadly Secrets of Jersey's Wartime Tunnels
1943

Rows of bunk beds, neatly made, stood empty in the silence of the dark wards in this strange sub-terranean world with its bricked up skeletons and disappearing railway lines.

There is an excellent book, *German Tunnels in the Channel Islands* (M Ginns, Channel Islands Occupation Society, 1993), which gives details of all the tunnels excavated in the Islands, blasted out of the rock and often lined with great precision, by the Germans, or, to be more precise, by their slave workers. Although the book is very factual and informative there are nevertheless eerie undertones. Why did the Germans choose to tunnel so extensively into the Islands? Guy Walters has written a suspenseful and equally eerie novel entitled *The Occupation* in which the tunnels on Alderney hid the manufacture of some new and deadly weapon. This did in fact happen, but in France, not on Alderney. There have long been rumours that the plan of the underground hospital on Guernsey matched the plan of the gas chambers at Auschwitz rather more than that of a hospital but this is all mere conjecture. The basic practicalities of such a project are more against than for the establishment of such facilities. However, there still does not seem to be any rational explanation for the Germans behaving like moles in the Islands.

Jersey was the island where the idea of underground tunnels had first been proposed and discussed by the Germans in 1941 and it subsequently became the first island into which the Germans tunnelled. The word 'tunnel' comes from the German language but the Channel Island tunnels were always referred to as

Hohlgangsanlegen which literally translated means 'a cave passage installation'. They were called *Ho* for short and each was given a number. The unlined tunnels are very similar to caves; the lined ones are like spacious railway tunnels. The standard of the tunnel building on Jersey was generally higher than on Guernsey or Alderney and the underground tunnel system was more complete. The Germans built a network of tunnels beneath the island for storing food supplies, ammunition and military equipment. In many of them railways were built to give ease of movement for the various commodities. On a lighter note the even temperature in the tunnels made them good wine cellars. No point in having these valuable commodities above ground where they would be vulnerable to bombing by Allied planes. This same principle, the Germans realised, could also apply to troops, and the idea of the underground hospital was born.

By 1943 the tide of the War had begun to turn against the Germans. Despite the Führer's bluster some serious European battles were seen as imminent by the High Command and German officers had to face the fact that there would probably be heavy German casualties. Desperately anxious to hold the Channel Islands the Germans had fortified them heavily and they now began to see the Islands as a good place to bring wounded troops for recovery. Jersey being closest to the coast of France, where it was expected that most such battles would take place, was singled out for the building of the first underground hospital. There was not time for the building of such a resource to be carried out from scratch and so it was decided that one of the existing tunnels would be adapted and fitted out as a field hospital.

Ho8 in St Lawrence was a tunnel system originally built to house a complex of artillery workshops. It had then proved necessary to blast and remove 14,000 tons of unstable shale rock to build two 200 yard long parallel tunnels and six shorter connecting tunnels for conversion to a hospital. Slave labour was used for this; mostly Russians from the Ukraine and Spanish Republican freedom fighters whom General Franco, for reasons unknown, had specifically requested the Führer to send to the Channel Islands. All these men were badly treated by the Germans who hated the Russians for their prowess against Germany in the war, while the Spanish Republicans had been declared stateless by Franco and were therefore not subject to any of the international conventions for treatment of prisoners. They were beaten and starved and scant

Ho8 German tunnel in St Lawrence, which was converted to an underground hospital. Several of the workers who built it are entombed here. The author

regard was paid to health and safety regulations during the blasting of the tunnels. A Spanish worker lost a leg when it was sliced off by a falling sheet of corrugated iron and he subsequently bled to death. Three workers were killed in one rock fall; twenty-two died in another rock fall. It was considered too dangerous to retrieve all the dead and some bodies were left where they fell, entombed in the rock and cement of this grim place.

The underground hospital is the only tunnel system in Jersey with corners built at right angles rather than as curves. Eerily, 60 cm gauge railway lines disappear beneath blank walls. These are the remnants of an internal railway system built to serve the artillery workshops. During the hospital conversion unfinished tunnels were bricked up and converted into wards, the lines disappearing into the darkness beyond the walls. The hospital included wards, an operating theatre, consulting rooms, a field kitchen, bathrooms, store rooms, and a mortuary. There was an efficient central heating system with large pipes and a huge boiler, a now unique air filtration plant, and internal electrical and telephone systems. Rows of bunk beds, neatly made, stood empty in the silence of the dark wards in this strange subterranean world with its bricked up skeletons and disappearing railway lines. It is the stuff of ghosts and hauntings and Alfred Hitchcock would have felt at home there.

In the event the underground hospital turned out to be little used for treating wounded soldiers and those that were treated often emerged looking worse than when they were brought in. The reasons for this were lack of natural light, sunlight and fresh air plus dampness in the tunnels, and the spooky sensations of such a place. The Jersey Underground Hospital can still be visited and it is open on most days. However, an hour or so spent in the dimly lit tunnels with their brooding atmosphere is enough for most visitors who are often visibly relieved to be back in broad daylight. Modern nurses shiver at the thought of having to work in such a place. The notion of days or even weeks incarcerated in such a place was not something to be imagined with any pleasure by patients either, even with the promise of recovery from injury, but was rather to be faced with foreboding and perhaps even dread. Ho16 was built in St Peter as a further shelter for German personnel. The slave workers would be left to take their chances.

Ironically the underground hospital was situated in the parish of St Lawrence. St Lawrence earned his sainthood by being roasted alive on a grid for his beliefs and that grid is incorporated into the parish flag of St Lawrence to this day. In many ways it was an appropriate symbol of the hell in which many of the slave workers lived. There was a camp at Goose Green Marsh where these workers lived under the harsh regime imposed by the Organisation Todt who were responsible for overseeing the construction of the tunnels. It was from such a camp that Russian slave worker, Bill Buryiv, escaped (see Chapter 30). He and fellow inmates faced daily beatings, a starvation diet, lack of sanitation facilities, and Buryiv had no warm or clean clothes; but he was one of the lucky ones. He escaped.

St Lawrence appears, for some (possibly geological) reason to have been a popular place for tunnel building. Ho1 was built on La Route d'Aleval on the St Peter/St Lawrence border on the west side of the valley. It served as a munitions store and was on a herringbone-style of layout. The 'enigma' of Ho1 is that it was so huge and no one really knows why. Large areas are now blocked by rock falls and are said to contain extensive amounts of German military equipment which was buried after the war because the Allies did not know how else to get rid of such items. Jersey Mushroom Growers have now sealed off other parts 'for all time' as '. . . spores in the sealed areas are detrimental to mushroom growth . . .' No further details on the nature of these 'spores' has been given. Its neighbour, Ho2, lay on the eastern side of the valley and consisted of a series of small tunnels for ration storage. Ho2 has remained dark, locked and abandoned since the scrap metal drive of the 1950s (see below). What will future historians make of these tunnels and their possible uses?

On a lighter note, possibly the most unusual and probably unique reuse of a German war tunnel is that of Ho17 at Verclut Point in St Catherine's on the east coast. Ho17, known then as Gibraltar Rock, was originally intended as a store for munitions and military equipment with which the Germans expected to have to defend Jersey's east coast against attack from the Allies in

Ho17 German tunnel in St Martin, Jersey, now a fish farm. The author

St Peter's Bunker. Today, Jersey has learned to live with the memories of the German occupation, 1940–45. The author

France. There is a long breakwater and pier at St Catherine's and a view along picturesque cliffs to the Fliquet Tower and Fliquet Castle which could have come straight out of Bram Stoker's *Dracula*. At the land end of the breakwater is a modern café that appears to be a popular spot for Sunday brunches and around a corner next to the café lies Ho17. The external appearance has not changed but there is a large sign proclaiming 'Jersey Turbot' over the entrance and an information board explains that this particular tunnel is now home to a fish farm. Reading the details it is obvious that the fish enjoy a much better quality of life than the wretched slave labour force who built the tunnel under their cruel German overlords.

After the war many of the other tunnels were filled with German military equipment and sealed in 1946 'for all eternity'. All eternity lasted for about five years until the post war scrap metal drive of the 1950s. Ho2, also in St Lawrence, was officially reopened in 1972. Here the relics of war included a German field kitchen, military equipment, a gun carriage and thousands of German helmets. Today, a few tunnels are still in use, mainly as storage units. Ho19 is used by the Harbour Electricity Generating Board. It is important to remember that most of these tunnels stand in private land and several are extremely dangerous and unstable. It may be possible to enter some of them but advice should first be sought from staff at Jersey Museum in St Helier, from the Jersey Underground Hospital in St Lawrence, or from the Channel Islands Occupation Society in St Ouen, Jersey.

CHAPTER 33

Witching Times
19th & 20th centuries

... this silly belief, once so common in the world, is now but rarely heard of, and that only among the most ignorant and besotted of mankind ...

Some say it is hard to understand how, surrounded by the marvels of twentieth century technology, people could still believe so strongly in the power of witchcraft, but there is in all of us a deep seated tendency to superstition. It is so much an accepted part of life that it often goes unremarked. For instance, almost everyone has said 'touch wood' at some point when they feel they have said something that might tempt fate. Leave a ladder leaning against a wall and watch how many people will walk round it, not under it, even when, as in busy town centres, walking under it the safer option. There is a marked reluctance to board trains and boats and planes on Friday the 13th. Major airports and seaports note a distinct fall in travelling numbers when Friday falls on the 13th of a month. Friday, of course, was the witches' Sabbath and thirteen the unlucky number at the Last Supper. Perhaps all this makes it easier to understand why Jersey, comparatively isolated and old fashioned until after the Second World War, could carry a strong belief in witchcraft right into modern times.

Witchcraft is hard to define but a major common denominator in all centuries has been the preparation of pills, potions and herbal remedies to ease various ailments. Yet people do not think that chemists/pharmacists, who sell St John's Wort for depression, or the aptly named witch hazel for healing wounds, are witches. The drug company, who organised the infamous drug trials that left several volunteers fighting for their lives, was called a number of names but 'witch' wasn't one of them. A witch is usually someone

Devil's Hole, near Priory Inn, *c. 1920.* Author's collection

who has deep instinctive sensibilities and sensitivities as well as a knowledge of herbal uses and medicines. His, or more usually her, natural 'vibes' allow him or her to empathise with those who seek their help. As they have these enhanced abilities people naturally assume that it will give them power over others and this is often what causes the problems.

That is the rational explanation, but Jersey wasn't always for listening to it. On 7 November 1835 a case was brought before the Royal Court of Jersey that three young men were charged with having gone into a field in Grouville parish where a lady named Molly Gallichan was milking her cow and threatening to kill her if she did not restore the health of their bewitched sister. Finally one of the men, John Le Viscount, told the others to let her alone because '... she had not long to live now in any case ...'

Molly Gallichan's defence counsel, Advocate Godfrey, told the Court that the brothers, Charles and Philip Aubin, and their friend, John le Viscount, still believed in witches and witchcraft. Molly, although not a qualified medical practitioner, was treating Esther, the sister of Charles and Philip Aubin, with various potions, mainly herbal. However, the girl had a serious long term illness and when she did not recover quickly Charles and Philip denounced Molly as a witch.

As no physical harm had been done to anyone the Royal Court simply bound the three men over in the sum of ten pounds and told them to be more sensible in future. The *Jersey Argus*, however, was not about to let them off so lightly and subjected them to public ridicule. On 17 November 1835, in an article on the case, the paper commented:

> ... *this silly belief* [in witchcraft], *once so common in the world, is now but rarely heard of, and then only among the most ignorant and besotted of mankind* ...

Two decades later, however, in 1855, there was a similar occurrence in the parish of St Ouen. A wealthy farmer had become rather too fond of the bottle and frequently drank himself into a stupor. His hangovers were something terrible and his health started to deteriorate. Rather than face facts, the farmer decided he had been bewitched and looked round for someone to blame. His bleary eyes alighted on his next door neighbour, an honest hard-working market gardener and smallholder. The farmer, pretending friendship, asked the unsuspecting man to take a look at something

Devil sculpture, close to Priory Inn, *above the collapsed cave system known as The Devil's Hole.* The author

in one of his barns. Once in the barn, the farmer slammed and bolted the doors, took a heavy cart whip down from a hook and beat his neighbour to within an inch of his life.

While most stories of witchcraft 'spells' are explainable, there are some that are not. The most frequent inexplicable occurrence on Jersey, was lice infestation. There are far too many accounts of it happening to be just dismissed. The following story from St Lawrence is a perfect illustration. A farmer named Jean was selling some land which would make him quite a rich man. A certain Saturday was appointed as the day on which he should go to the

Royal Court in St Helier to sign contracts. A day or so before he was due to depart a local tramp came to his door asking for a pot of cider. The farmer told him to go away. The tramp said quietly that Jean had a choice. Give him the pot of cider he requested or lose his contract because he would never get to the Royal Court in time to sign it. The farmer scoffed at him and sent him on his way without the cider.

On the Saturday morning Jean dressed carefully in his best clothes. It was an important day for him. It was a lovely morning and he set off in good spirits. However by the time he had reached the top of Mont Conchon his head and neck were itching and the skin on his face was blotchy and irritated. The itching got worse and finally in desperation Jean took off his collar to try and ease it. To his horror his collar was covered in lice. Then he looked down at his clothes. He was crawling with lice from head to foot. Hot, uncomfortable and ashamed, Jean turned round and made for home, walking across the fields to avoid meeting anyone. He had to wash and change before he could present himself in public at the court. He knew he was late as he ran across the grass, stumbling and breathless. When he finally reached his house he let himself in a back door and hurried upstairs. Once in his bedroom he began to strip off his clothes but he was amazed to see that there was not a single louse visible anywhere. Jean's mouth dropped open in astonishment and then he recalled the words of the disgruntled tramp. His prediction had come true. Jean had refused to give the tramp his cider and now Jean had lost his contract and his profit as a result.

Far fetched as it may sound there are hundreds of similar stories. There were often eyewitnesses and it is difficult to explain all the instances as the results of overworked imaginations, self delusions or mass hysteria. Some cases even made it to the Royal Court. There is nothing to suggest that Jersey, or Guernsey for that matter which had just as many instances of lice infestation, is a hotbed for breeding louses. At the same time something must have happened. Perhaps one day forensic science, or a science of the future, will provide the answers. For now the Jersiaise called it witchcraft.

The last trial for witchcraft on Guernsey took place in 1914. Jersey went one better and their last trial for witchcraft took place on the island in 1932. It concerned a thirty-four-year-old fortune teller. Reading the future may be improbable, but it is not usually classed as a crime, and people have been having their fortunes told since the days of the Romans. However, his mistake was to tell one woman, who had paid him good money, to get in touch with her brother because she would learn something to her advantage. Her brother was dead and, somewhat disenchanted, she called the police and demanded her money back. The case went to the Royal Court and when the fortune teller was called to the stand to take the oath he greatly surprised the people saying, 'I swear by Allah'. He was subsequently sentenced to nine months hard labour for 'black magic'.

It might be thought that the German Occupation and the advent of the Technological Age would have ended the belief in witchcraft once and for all but that is not the case at all. Today, ironically, there is a 'witchcraft shop' in St Helier which sells books on the occult, white magic and black magic, witchcraft, spells, tarot cards; and all manner of 'New Age' charms, potions and posters. The wheel appears to have turned full circle.

TRUE CRIME FROM WHARNCLIFFE

Foul Deeds and Suspicious Deaths Series

Barking, Dagenham & Chadwell Heath
Barnsley
Bath
Bedford
Birmingham
More Foul Deeds Birmingham
Black Country
Blackburn and Hyndburn
Bolton
Bradford
Brighton
Bristol
Cambridge
Carlisle
Chesterfield
Cumbria
More Foul Deeds Chesterfield
Colchester
Coventry
Croydon
Derby
Durham
Ealing
Fens
Folkstone and Dover
Grimsby
Guernsey
Guildford
Halifax
Hampstead, Holborn and St Pancras

Huddersfield
Hull
Jersey
Leeds
Leicester
Lewisham and Deptford
Liverpool
London's East End
London's West End
Manchester
Mansfield
More Foul Deeds Wakefield
Newcastle
Newport
Norfolk
Northampton
Nottingham
Oxfordshire
Pontefract and Castleford
Portsmouth
Rotherham
Scunthorpe
Southend-on-Sea
Southport
Staffordshire and the Potteries
Stratford and South Warwickshire
Tees
Warwickshire
Wigan
York

OTHER TRUE CRIME BOOKS FROM WHARNCLIFFE

A-Z of London Murders
A-Z of Yorkshire Murders
Black Barnsley
Brighton Crime and Vice 1800-2000
Durham Executions
Essex Murders
Executions & Hangings in Newcastle
    and Morpeth
Norfolk Mayhem and Murder

Norwich Murders
Strangeways Hanged
Unsolved Murders in Victorian &
    Edwardian London
Unsolved Norfolk Murders
Unsolved Yorkshire Murders
Warwickshire's Murderous Women
Yorkshire Hangmen
Yorkshire's Murderous Women

Please contact us via any of the methods below for more information
or a catalogue
WHARNCLIFFE BOOKS
47 Church Street, Barnsley, South Yorkshire, S70 2AS
Tel: 01226 734555 • 734222 • Fax: 01226 734438
email: enquiries@pen-and-sword.co.uk
website: www.wharncliffebooks.co.uk

Index